52 Simple
Things
You Can Do
To Be
Pro-Life

SECONDS

52 Simple Things You Can Do To Be Pro-Life

ANNE PIERSON

and Carol Risser

BETHANY HOUSE PUBLISHERS

MINNEAPOLIS, MINNESOTA 55438

Published by Bethany House Publishers
A Ministry of Bethany Fellowship, Inc.
6820 Auto Club Road, Minneapolis, Minnesota 55438

Printed in the United States of America

Library of Congress Cataloging-in-Publication Data

Pierson, Anne.
    52 simple things you can do to be pro-life / Anne Pierson, Carol Risser.
        p. cm.

    1. Abortion—Religious aspects—Christianity. 2. Pro-life movement—United States—Handbooks, manuals, etc. I. Title. II. Title: Fifty-two ways you can be pro-life (without getting arrested)
HQ767.25.P54   1990
241'.6976—dc20   90-45481
ISBN 1-55661-170-6   CIP

We dedicate this book to the thousands of wonderful people
we have met who have provided a pinch of salt.

May you be as much of an inspiration to those who read this
book as you have been to us!

ANNE PIERSON, Executive Director of Loving and Caring, Inc., is considered a "grandmother" of the pro-life movement by many. Part of the first wave of people to provide services for unwed mothers, she and her husband Jim started their first pro-life ministry in 1973. As the author of several other pro-life books, she speaks at retreats and conferences regularly. She and her family make their home in Pennsylvania.

CAROL RISSER has served at Loving and Caring since it started in 1984. She is involved with Presbyterians Pro-Life and has served on the boards of several local pro-life ministries. At Loving and Caring, she has helped produce many aids for counseling pregnant women as well as manuals for setting up maternity homes and extended family living programs. She and her husband live in Pennsylvania.

Contents

A Pinch of Salt   9

Part I ■ 52 Simple Things

1. Pray for a Pro-Life Ministry.   11
2. Offer to Baby-Sit for a Single Parent or the Parents of a
   Handicapped Child   12
3. Don't Apologize—Advertise.   13
4. Make Your Voice Heard in the Political Arena   14
5. March for Life.   16
6. Collect and Donate Pro-Life Books to Your Church.   18
7. Hold a Garage Sale.   19
8. Start a Pro-Life File of Magazine and News Stories.   20
9. Volunteer Your Computer for a Pro-Life Cause   20
10. Offer Your Office Skills   22
11. Wear a "Precious Feet" Pin   23
12. Speak Out for Chastity   23
13. Offer Your Professional Services   25
14. Collect Food for a Pro-Life Housing Ministry   27
15. Be a Special Friend/Advocate for a Single Mother   28
16. Remember a Single Parent on Special Occasions   30
17. Volunteer at Your Pregnancy Counseling Center.   31
18. Pass on Your Unique Gifts to Women at a Maternity Home . .   32
19. Be a Foster Parent for an Adoption Agency.   33
20. Serve on the Board of a Pro-Life Ministry.   34
21. Talk to a Friend About Your Feelings   35
22. Help Your Child With School and Book Reports   36
23. Become Involved With Handicapped People   37
24. Bake a Treat   38
25. Become the Pro-Life Contact Person for Your Church   39
26. Invite Someone From a Pro-Life Ministry to Speak   40
27. Invite a Pro-Life Speaker to Your School.   41
28. Help Make Young Women in a Maternity Home Feel
    Welcome.   42
29. Give Financially   43
30. Subscribe to Publications.   45

31. Make a Name for Yourself in the Media................... 46
32. Give a Party!... 48
33. Be a Labor Coach for a Single Pregnant Woman........... 49
34. Mend/Make Clothing for a Pro-Life Ministry.............. 50
35. Host a Baby Shower...................................... 51
36. Organize or Participate in "Work Days" at a Pro-Life
    Ministry.. 52
37. Picket an Abortion Clinic 53
38. Investigate What Your Schools Are Teaching
    About Sexuality and Offer Them Alternatives 55
39. Sponsor a Pro-Life Writing Contest..................... 56
40. Write or Sponsor a Pamphlet 57
41. Walk or Sponsor Someone in a "Walk-A-Thon" 57
42. Talk to Your Doctor 59
43. Shop Garage Sales/Thrift Stores 60
44. Participate in or Start a Pro-Life Sunday at Your Church ... 61
45. "Back Up" Houseparents................................. 62
46. Help Your Church or Pro-Life Group Sponsor a Sexuality
    Seminar... 64
47. Organize or Participate in a Life Chain................. 65
48. Compile a List of Materials and Resources for Your
    Denomination.. 66
49. Show a Pro-Life Film or Video 68
50. Start a Civics Committee at Your Church 69
51. Enhance Self-Image, and Make a Memory 70
52. Remember Senior Citizens.............................. 72

Part II ■ Things Requiring More Involvement

53. Start a Support Group for Women Who Have Had
    Abortions 74
54. Consider Adopting a "Special-Needs" Child.............. 75
55. Be an Extended Family to a Young Woman in Need 76
56. Run for Political Office................................ 78
57. Plan a Pro-Life Career 80
58. Consider a Career Change 81
59. Serve as Houseparents in a Pro-Life Housing
    Ministry.. 83
Loving and Caring: Who Are We? 85
Appendix A: Local / National Resources 87
Appendix B: 52-Item List 91
Appendix C: Key Scriptures Concerning Abortion 92

A Pinch of Salt

How important it is that we realize the pro-life movement is far broader in scope than saving unborn babies and helping women who are experiencing a crisis pregnancy! Certainly, both are very important aspects of our work and ministry. Yet they are pieces of a much larger whole.

Over the years, we have seen firsthand the length, width, height and depth of the pro-life movement. The term "pro-life" encompasses ministry to single parents struggling to raise children alone, and to the handicapped for whom life is a lonely battle. These people, all created and loved by God, are as much in need of the pro-life movement as mothers and babies.

Because of this vast scope of human need, the pro-life movement can involve us all. Everyone—especially we who are the body of Christ—can be doing something that is pro-life. Children, grandparents, mothers and fathers; our churches, businesses, youth groups, classrooms, Bible studies and prayer groups—all can play a simple but *vital* role in this move of God that is sweeping our country.

Perhaps you have wondered, *what can I do in the pro-life movement that will make a difference? What can I do that will have an impact and make a change?* The ideas presented here are simple—but each one is like a cleansing, preserving touch of salt. Jesus doesn't ask that you be a whole box of salt—only a pinch of it (Matthew 5:13). Will you be salt?

We can reach out in our own way, according to the particular call God has put on our lives—and in reaching out, we can draw others closer to God. Men, women, and children all around us cry out for loving, caring hands. And in ways that are simple and natural, we can bring the kingdom of God to them.

No task or gift is too small to help win God's battle on behalf of mankind. This book was conceived to encourage and to help you take your rightful place in this battle. We know that with each gift of service you offer, you will find blessing.

Anne Pierson
Carol Risser

Part One:
52 Simple Things

| 1 |

Pray for a Pro-Life Ministry

The power of prayer works! Every ministry that exists needs God's grace and *your* prayers.

There are very few areas in the United States that don't have some active pro-life group ministering through crisis-pregnancy counseling, or a maternity home, or Christian adoption counseling. By calling or writing them, you can ask to be included on their mailing list in order to be kept abreast of their activities and needs. Some ministries have prayer letters or calendars they send out upon request, so be sure they include you on this as well.

When You Pray:

- Pray for the clients, that their hearts would be tender and open to receive counsel and the love and forgiveness of God.
- Pray for the director and all those in decision-making positions, such as the ministry's board of directors.
- Pray for the wisdom of God's Holy Spirit; for unity among the staff members; for the marriages and families of all staff and volunteers.
- Pray for their funding efforts and that people would be touched to give generously and regularly.
- Keep individual prayer requests on a calendar in your kitchen

and involve your family in praying for these daily needs as well.

Prayer has opened doors of ministry to hurting people, rejuvenated funding, and, in one case we know, been a mighty spiritual weapon that helped to shut down a local abortion clinic for lack of business! (See 2 Corinthians 10:4.)

Time: As much as you'd like to devote.
Cost: Nothing.

See National Resources: 14.

2

Offer to Baby-Sit for a Single Parent or the Parents of a Handicapped Child

For single parents or parents who have a handicapped child requiring special care, finding baby sitters they can afford or who are willing to cope with their child's needs can be very difficult. Fortunately, baby-sitting can be done by anyone—from teenager through grandparent, by a single person, a couple, a man or woman. This love gift takes only a few hours of your time and a willing heart.

Catherine is a single mom who works full time and is the parent of an eight-year-old boy named Jesse. When Jesse is in school, her schedule is relatively easy to manage, but summers create a problem with baby-sitting, which can be very expensive. Wendy, a young mother in Catherine's church, became aware of her need and offered to keep Jesse at her home during the summer while Catherine worked. Wendy's husband also took a special interest in Jesse and has taken him fishing, to a baseball game, and to an air show. Summer turns out to be very special for Jesse, Catherine, and Wendy's entire family.

Jim, a dad with two grown daughters, offers to baby-sit for David from time to time. He works with David's mom, who also goes to the same church as Jim and his wife. Sometimes there are functions for the ladies of the church, and Jim has found he can help out by spending an evening with David while his mom attends the outings with Jim's wife. Jim and David are becoming special friends in the process. Jim always greets David at church, asks him how his week is going, or what he did at school recently. And David's mom usually leaves a special treat for "the boys" when Jim comes to baby-sit.

Free up others who want to serve.

By offering to baby-sit, you may actually free someone else to minister. Mark and Mary loved young people and wanted to work with the Monday night youth group at their church, but they had a handicapped child. In order to be able to run youth meetings, they needed a dependable sitter. A newlywed couple in their church heard about the need and offered to come to their home on Monday evenings to sit with their child. Everyone received a blessing from the arrangement, and a special relationship was formed between the two couples.

Baby-sitting falls in the definition of pro-life work because it involves loving some of God's very special people.

Time: A few hours, or a full day.
Cost: Nothing.

See Local Resources: 2, 7.

3

Don't Apologize—Advertise

Early Christians used the sign of a fish to symbolize their Christian beliefs. When other Christians saw the sign, they were encouraged and knew they were talking to a brother or sister in Jesus. Likewise, when we see pro-life messages on others' correspondence or vehicles, *we* are encouraged. We also encourage others with our pro-life messages.

Have you considered that there are many different ways to let others know you are pro-life? Get a stamp or pro-life stickers for your correspondence and, when appropriate, use them on envelopes that go out of your home or business.

Consider having a pro-life message—"Choose Life" or "Pray to End Abortion"—put on your checks. Turn your car into a pro-life billboard with your favorite pro-life bumper sticker.

T-shirts are another excellent means for getting across *any* point. Why not use your families' T-shirts to get out a pro-life message? There are many available, and if you would like to produce your own, this can also be done through many shopping mall T-shirt outlets. For resources, see the Appendix.

Time: Minimal.
Cost: From nothing to several dollars for a stamp or pro-life stickers, to around $10 for a T-shirt.

See Local Resources: 5.
National Resources: 12, 17, 19.

4

Make Your Voice Heard in the Political Arena

When a politician is pro-abortion, you have to wonder if they truly understand the meaning of our nation's Declaration of Independence: "We hold these truths to be self-evident, that *all men* are created equal, that they are endowed by their Creator with certain inalienable *rights*, that among these are *life*, liberty, and the pursuit of happiness. . . ." It sounds as if our founding fathers were both God-fearing *and* pro-life!

Here are three important needs requiring varying commitments of time and resources.

Vote pro-life.

One way we can be pro-life in our community is to vote pro-life, sending powerful signals to our local and state representatives. Be sure that your state pro-life Political Action Committee has your name on their mailing list so that you can receive news about both pro-life and pro-abortion candidates. (A contribution from time to time will help your P.A.C.'s do their job.)

Time: Approximately one hour prior to each election to read literature from the candidates.

Cost: An occasional contribution to a pro-life Political Action Committee to remain on their mailing list.

Write to elected officials.

Take time to encourage those politicians who are pro-life. Purchase twelve post cards and each month send one politician a brief note, telling them you appreciate (or don't appreciate) their stand for the unborn. Many of the organizations listed in the Appendix regularly publish legislative alerts.

Time: A few minutes to a half hour each month to write your card.

Cost: A couple dollars for twelve post cards purchased from the post office.

Become a party committee person.

Get to know about your local committeeman or woman, and if they are not pro-life, collect signatures and run as a pro-life candidate in the primary election. It is the committeemen and women who elect the party chairmen. A majority of pro-life committee people will help elect pro-life chairmen from your state.

Orpha, a young Christian woman who works for a building contractor, won election as a committee person the first time around as a write-in candidate *with only 83 votes.* The campaign cost her very little money. In her second election, she spent approximately $350 on flyers and postage, since she had to compete with the publicity of her opponent. Again she won, by a margin of 235 to 84.

We realize that for many readers becoming a party committee person or actually running for office is moving beyond the "simple ways" of pro-life involvement. We include it here because for some, these will be a natural step up in their involvement.

Time: Time spent running for committee person varies, depending on whether or not you are opposed by another candidate. Fifteen signatures are required to place yourself on the ballot as a committeeman or woman. The candidate usually arranges to spend election day at the polls. Being a committee person requires approximately one week a year, plus whatever time it takes to stay informed about the issues.

Cost: Varies, depending on whether or not you are running opposed.

See Local Resources: 4.
National Resources: 2, 6, 8, 10, 11, 22.

5

March for Life

Sometimes we are overwhelmed by all the opportunities to voice our support for the pro-life movement. The first half of 1990 alone included the annual March for Life on January 22, a Rally for Life in April at the Washington Monument, and a Unity '90 video telecast in June, all sponsored and promoted by different pro-life groups. No doubt it's impossible for you to attend all the public pro-life gatherings.

Nonetheless, as a committed person you *can* help by (1) attending public demonstrations, marches and events whenever possible; (2) helping to publicize local and national rallies in the public marketplace; and (3) praying for those gatherings when you can't attend in person.

What is it like to march for life?

The annual march in Washington, sponsored by March for Life, has been around longest of all the public pro-life demonstrations. Faithful pro-life supporters have been meeting on January 22, the anniversary of the Supreme Court's *Roe* v. *Wade* pro-abortion decision, since 1974. The march includes school children, entire families, the old as well as the very young, representing many religious faiths. Those who attend find the march is peaceful and are always encouraged to be part of such a large grass-roots movement.

Buses and carloads of people from all over the country arrive the morning of the march. The group gathers at noon on the ellipse in front of the White House to hear speeches from pro-life politicians, religious leaders, athletes and celebrities, and leaders of a variety of national pro-life organizations.

Afterward, the march begins, taking pro-lifers from the Ellipse to the Supreme Court building, slightly more than a mile away. Marchers are urged to take advantage of being in Washington by making an appointment to visit their U.S. representatives to express their views. They return to their buses or cars around dinnertime.

In 1976 a pro-life group in St. Louis, Missouri, sent one bus to the March for Life. In 1990 they had a contingent consisting of 26 buses and 1200 people. The trip from St. Louis generally lasts about 22 hours and marchers sleep en route, arriving the morning of the march to lobby their legislators, and marching and lobbying again in the afternoon. The organizer for St. Louis says the annual march "charges up the group to work for pro-life issues the rest of the year."

If no one sends buses from your church, city or town, why not consider renting one and getting together a group of people to attend? (For details on March for Life, check the Appendix.) Those who are too far away to attend the march in Washington can still seize the opportunity to march locally, in their own city or in their state capitol. Our numbers may not always be publicly acknowledged in the national news media, but you can be certain the legislators are well aware of our presence!

Time: Anywhere from several hours to a couple days, depending upon your driving distance to Washington or your state capitol.

Cost: Also depends upon your distance. In surrounding states, marchers generally pay around $15 to $20 apiece for a seat on a chartered bus and pack a lunch to eat on the way. (The St. Louis trip, for instance, costs each marcher about $85, plus meals.)

See Local Resources: 3.
National Resources: March for Life
                             Box 90300
                             Washington, DC 20090

| 6 |

Collect and Donate Pro-Life Books to Your Church

Educating the public often starts with your own church family. Many church people from mainline Protestant denominations state that they are pro-choice, either because their denomination has influenced them to think pro-choice, or perhaps because they have never been fully informed on all the facts of abortion. Thankfully, more and more of these denominations are beginning to rethink their previous pro-abortion stands. Within the last year, several voted to soften their hard-line pro-choice stand, and several other denominations have appointed study committees to examine the issue.

One way you help educate your church is by donating pro-life books to your church's lending library. A committee can be formed for this purpose, raising funds through bake or craft sales, then using the proceeds to purchase informative pro-life books. Or certain individuals may be willing to donate money specifically toward this purchase.

We recommend that a basic pro-life library consist of at least one book explaining the pro-life position, one short Christian novel or testimony about a teenager who becomes pregnant, and an adult novel or testimony on the same subject. Contact your Christian bookstore or book distributor for help. They will have a selection of pro-life books for you to peruse before you make your purchase.

You may also want to include the names and addresses of your local pro-life ministries in the front or back of the book, in case book borrowers want to become further involved.

Another way you can help with books is to donate funds to your local pro-life ministry so they can purchase books or pamphlets to use in their counseling. Some regularly use counseling workbooks, others have resources on parenting that they like to give their clients. Maternity homes like to keep a resource of good pro-life reading material on hand which, from time to time, must be replenished.

Time: Minimal for selecting books.
Cost: About $4 to $10 per book.

See Local Resources: 5, 6.
National Resources: 3, 9, 19, 21.

7

Hold a Garage Sale

You can accomplish several things at once with a pro-life garage sale: You can clean out your house by getting rid of some good but unneeded extra possessions; socialize and fellowship with friends; and you can help support a deserving pro-life ministry.

A recent, four-family garage sale sponsored by a neighborhood Bible study group lasted from 8:00 A.M. until 3:00 P.M. and raised a total of $200. A few preparational hours were spent going through attics and closets and in pricing items. One person was designated to operate the "cash box" and the others stood at their tables to answer questions. The only costs were advertising in the local newspaper and stick-on price labels. (As it turned out, the couples involved had as much fun buying each others' stuff as they had selling their possessions to strangers!)

Maybe your church's adult Sunday school class or a Bible study would consider sponsoring a flea market or garage sale on the church grounds. Of course, the more people involved, the more planning and preparation will be required.

If your group is donating the proceeds from the sale to more than one organization, you can have a table of literature on each ministry available for those who come to browse and buy. Or the person operating the cash box might simply hand a brochure to each customer.

Best-selling items at a garage or rummage sale include cheap used paperbacks, bedspreads and bed linens (purchased in the spring for vacation homes and campers!), children's clothing and toys, old silverware and glassware, working appliances, baby clothes and furnishings, sports and camping gear.

Time: About one to two days.
Cost: About $50 for advertising and labels.

See Local Resources: 3.

8

Start a Pro-Life File of Magazine and News Stories

In 1983, Carol and a group of concerned men and women from her church started a group that met to discuss the problem of abortion. To keep abreast of issues involving different social issues, they started collecting newspaper and magazine articles and saving them in manila files under topical headings.

The group has since disbanded, but Carol's article file continues to grow. She draws upon it when she speaks out against abortion, attends pro-life meetings, and often uses some of the facts she finds to dispute pro-abortion stories in her local media with letters to the editor. Even on the nights when she is too busy to read the entire paper, she finds herself quickly scanning headlines for articles affecting abortion and the family to clip and file. She believes having a long history of clippings helps her keep a perspective on the issues and always gives her a history to draw from in her letters. The Appendix includes resources available for building this file.

Time: A few minutes each evening to scan and clip; 30 minutes per month to file.

Cost: The price of your local newspaper, plus a couple dollars for manila folders and a file box (if you don't have a file).

See Local Resources: 9.
National Resources: All that are listed.

9

Volunteer Your Computer for a Pro-Life Cause

Bill and his wife have been active in pro-life work for a number of years—and Bill is a "gadget nut." When he bought his first computer for his home business, the couple saw a way they could dedicate part of its use to the Lord's work. They offered to maintain the mailing list for their local crisis pregnancy center.

For several years, they added new names as the list was built. They did the address changes and gave the center gummed mailing labels for their newsletter, along with a print-out on which they could make changes for the next mailing. They donated the cost of the mailing labels as well, which they purchased from a discount office products store.

When it came time to upgrade his home computer, Bill decided to donate the first computer to the center whose labels he'd been maintaining. Now the center has a personal computer for word processing and for their mailing list, and Bill has a tax deduction from the old computer.

Another way a home computer can be used is by helping to produce a newsletter or brochure for a ministry. If you have the capability to do desk-top publishing on your computer, you may save a local ministry several hundred dollars a year by volunteering to help with their newsletter or brochure. Ellen learned to do desk-top publishing at work, and her boss allows her to come to work early to use the equipment so that, on her own time, she helps a struggling ministry with their publishing needs.

Check with your local pro-life group, crisis pregnancy center or maternity home to see if they have a need. New ministries usually have the greatest need for this type of help.

Time: One to two hours for address changes and updates, several times a year, depending on how often the center's newsletter is mailed. Slightly longer to produce a newsletter or brochure, depending on your computer skills.

Cost: Gummed mailing labels can now be purchased for about $1.75 per thousand.

See Local Resources: 3.

| 10 |

Offer Your Office Skills

The staff of most ministries we know are underpaid and over-worked. Dealing with crises on a daily basis always takes precedence over typing, filing, filling out forms and managing the financial books.

A person with office, organizational or bookkeeping skills and a few hours a week to donate will find himself or herself welcomed with open arms by the staff of many ministries. Here are some examples.

- Deb organizes volunteers for a local maternity home. Starting with a collection of hurriedly scribbled notes, phone memos and forms, she organizes the volunteers by interest on color-coded index cards, and stores them in a file box for the housemother's quick reference.
- Rod and Judy, a retired couple, have helped out by labeling a maternity home's newsletters and stapling return envelopes inside.
- Brenda hand-addresses thank-you notes for the director of a local crisis pregnancy center.
- Carl helps make address changes for a pregnancy center on the center's own computer.
- Karen volunteered her knowledge of computer spreadsheets to help a ministry set up a budget spreadsheet and record expenses for its board meetings.

Contact your local pregnancy center, maternity home, pro-life lobby group, or adoption agency. Chances are, all of them accept volunteers.

Time: Anywhere from a few hours a week to a few hours a month.
Cost: Nothing.

See Local Resources: 1, 3, 4.

11

Wear a "Precious Feet" Pin

When Jeanine's mother joined her for lunch at a local restaurant, she asked, "What's that you're wearing on your jacket?" Jeanine explained the significance of the tiny pin she was wearing: The little silver feet were identical in size and shape to those of a baby ten weeks after conception. Immediately, her mother asked if she could have a pair to wear, too!

You seem to see the "Precious feet" pin wherever you go. Of course, they are rampant at pro-life rallies and seminars, but they appear in quite unexpected places as well. We've seen them on the lapels of salesmen, teenagers, secretaries and blue-collar workers alike.

The "Precious Feet" pin is sold mail-order by Virginia and Ellis Evers of Taylor, Arizona, who developed them in 1976. Since then, over 5 million have been distributed throughout the world! The feet are available in a variety of finishes as lapel pins, necklaces, earrings and charms. These folks also offer a line of other pro-life material. A complete catalog is free for the asking (see Appendix).

Time: None.
Cost: From about $1 for a gilt-finished lapel pin to $90 or $100 for 14k gold.

See National Resources: 12.

12

Speak Out for Chastity

Molly Kelly, a housewife and mother of eight, became a pro-life speaker after the untimely death of her physician husband, Jim. "After Jim's death, I missed him so much that I looked for some way I could carry on his work. I had never done any public speaking before, but I researched the pro-life issues on abortion and decided to get involved speaking out on an issue that Jim cared so much about."

Molly gave two talks her first year. Then, when her youngest child entered kindergarten, she started going into area schools to speak. The school engagements led to invitations to debate on radio and television in the Philadelphia area, and national exposure grew from there.

Then, in 1985, Molly became frustrated that she was not dealing with enough solutions. "I decided I had to back up and start addressing sexual responsibility," she says. "Sexual responsibility is the solution to most of the problems we talk about today: abortion, teen pregnancy, venereal diseases, AIDS, the harmful side effects of contraceptives. We need to control our bodies from within, not from without."

When Molly first started speaking on her new topic, she went back to her research. "I was convinced sexual responsibility was the answer, but I had to research the right words to get it across. I decided chastity was a positive word."

Since then Molly has spoken to over 20,000 teens a year in both Christian and public schools. "I've found it's easier to bring the chastity message into public schools than the anti-abortion message," she says. "When I speak, I try to leave teens feeling good about themselves. I want to let them know they can meet the challenge of being in control of their bodies."

Along with Jean Garton, author of the pro-life classic *Who Broke the Baby*, and a powerful pro-life speaker herself, Molly has formed a team to train others to speak out on chastity in churches, at meetings and in the public schools. They hope to be able to duplicate what they have been doing throughout the country by training others in pro-life speaking techniques. You might consider inviting them to your area for a training seminar. You can contact Molly Kelly and Jean Garton (Pennsylvanians for Human Life) at (215) 667-1191. For additional information on chastity curricula and materials, see the Appendix.

Time: As long as it takes to become thoroughly comfortable speaking in public, and as much time as you're willing to devote to public speaking.

Cost: Approximately $300 to $500 for materials to thoroughly research the issues. Speaker expenses, if you invite someone in to speak (expenses vary).

See Local Resources: 3, 8.
National Resources: 1, 2, 4, 6, 16, 20, 25, 26, 28.

$$\boxed{13}$$

Offer Your Professional Services

Many people have gifts that are sorely needed in the pro-life movement. While it is true that a primary need is for volunteer counselors and individuals to answer phones, almost every profession and skill are needed in some capacity.

Construction workers/contractors.

Maternity homes, pregnancy centers and any ministries that need building maintenance periodically require the services of carpenters, plumbers, heating/air conditioning specialists, electricians, dry wallers, roofers and painters. All these skills are needed to keep the facilities in good repair, to add on to existing buildings, or to modify buildings to make them accessible to the handicapped.

In the private sector, there are individuals whose homes have unfinished areas, such as attics or basements. These people would be willing to take someone in to live with them, but the time and expense of completing the additional living space is prohibitive.

Single parents are also candidates for help in this area. Many need home repairs, but can't afford to pay for professional services. All of these are areas in which individuals in the building trades can use their God-given gifts to bless others.

Auto mechanics.

Cars owned by ministries need regular maintenance and, often, expensive repairs. Single parents often need help maintaining their cars. It's a blessing to have someone capable on call who can look at a car, help change the oil, or offer to be an advocate to help them get a good deal on repair services.

Doctors, lawyers, dentists, ophthalmologists, chiropractors . . .

These professionals can offer services to a needy parent or to a maternity home.

Vicki was living with Jim and Anne and together they were visiting a young woman in the hospital who had just had her baby. Noticing a lovely picture on the wall, Anne commented, "Look at that great poster."

"What poster?"

Anne knew Vicki well enough to recall that her school grades had been very poor and that she rarely opened a book. Now the reason became clear: Vicki had a serious eye problem.

Vicki was examined by a local eye doctor, who determined that her eyesight was so poor she saw words only as a blur. The doctor contributed his time for the examination free of charge and sold Vicki eyeglasses at his cost. A whole new world opened up for Vicki as she began to read two or three books a week. Her grades improved, and for the first time in her life she became excited about her future.

Printers.

Printers are uniquely equipped to be able to offer services to a pro-life ministry since virtually all ministries print brochures and print and distribute newsletters. One printer provided all the printing for a maternity home for many years. In appreciation, a ministry can acknowledge the services of their printer with a small credit line or ad in their material.

Bookkeepers and accountants.

Gathering figures for the annual audit and even paying bills on a week-to-week basis can be a time-consuming task for a small ministry staff. Someone with gifts in the financial area can volunteer to relieve them of this necessary burden.

Do you have a special skill you can offer? Call your local pro-life ministry or let your church know of your willingness to be used as God's vessel.

Time: Whatever you are willing to offer.
Cost: As much or as little of your valuable, professional time as you are willing to give.

See Local Resources: 1, 2, 3, 7.

14

Collect Food for a Pro-Life Housing Ministry

Three meals a day, seven days a week! In any type of housing program, good nutritious meals have to appear like clockwork. In a maternity housing program the need increases because of the special nutritional needs of pregnant women. And single-parent programs must deal with the special needs of children as well as mothers.

At the maternity home where Anne and Jim were houseparents, a car drove into the driveway one hot summer day. In the trunk was a bushel of peaches. Each young woman first enjoyed a fresh peach. Anne then organized baking parties. The women were divided into teams. Each team made pie crust (a first for some), and a production line of peach pies soon went into the ovens. As the pies baked, the teams agreed they would keep a few pies for the home and give away the rest—one to a widower, one to a needy family in the neighborhood, and so forth.

How can you help? Many people feel they have to purchase a whole bag of groceries (or a whole bushel of peaches!) in order to make a difference. Nothing is further from the truth. Too often we back off from helping because we fear we can't help in a big enough way.

One way to collect that bag of groceries in small increments is by using a 52-item list (see Appendix B). This is a list of the most-often consumed products in a typical housing program—gelatin, spaghetti sauce, cereal, canned goods, cake mixes, tuna. By following the 52-item list, a person can pick up one or two items as she shops each week, adding it to her own groceries. When a bag or two is filled, it can be dropped off at the ministry.

Once you develop the habit yourself, share the list with a friend, offering your home as the central collection point. If you belong to a women's or men's group, or Sunday school class, you can have the entire group take on the project and see how fast the bags fill. It is amazing how one or two items a week can make a tremendous dent in a housing ministry's grocery bill.

Time: No extra time for the 52-item list, except for occasional delivery
of groceries to the home.

Cost: Average $2 to $4 per week.

See Local Resources: 1, 3.

15

Be a Special Friend/Advocate for a Single Mother

Single parenting can occur because of many reasons. Sometimes
a young woman who is not married has one or more children. Sometimes she has been divorced by her husband, is widowed, or her husband may be in prison. A single father can be a widower, or may have
been deserted by his wife. The circumstances are not the issue. What
matters to God is how we choose to help this special family unit.

The Bible is very clear that we are to care for the fatherless and help
provide for their needs. Isaiah 1:17 says, "Learn to do right!. . . Defend
the cause of the fatherless!" When there is no father present, it is
important that men in the body of Christ are available to respond to
these children.

You probably already know a single parent through your church,
work place, or neighborhood. Chances are he or she will have children
of varying ages.

Keep in touch regarding their needs.

Vance and Vicki live in a town house in a suburban development.
Melissa and her daughter Melinda live in the same block and go to
their church. Vance and Vicki make a point to check in on them regularly to take care of any special needs Melissa may have around the
house. Recently, Vance installed a hanging lamp in her kitchen. Sometimes they invite Melissa and Melinda to share a meal or picnic with
their family. They have become good friends and everyone is blessed,
including Vance and Vicki's children, who are learning about caring
by watching their parents.

Time: A few hours a month.
Cost: Nothing.

Include a youngster in your family outings.

Ask a single-parent family to join you on family picnics or for special holiday meals. Consider including the child of a single parent in your plans when you take your own kids to a ball game or theme park. For example:

- Dewey takes a special interest in his young neighbor, Bryan. Each year, he plans a special outing such as a baseball game to attend together. He also makes it a point to spend time talking to Bryan when he sees him outside.
- Ike and Lena, the parents of two children, saved up their money and included a single mother and her son when they went on vacation to a Christian family camp. They paid for their entire stay.
- John and Ann, regular Christian camp-goers, found they were unable to attend their Christian camp one year due to a scheduling conflict. They decided they would take the money they would have spent on the camp and use it to sponsor a single parent and her three children. If you are part of a Bible study or Sunday school class, why not consider sponsoring a trip to a Christian family camp for a single parent and his or her children?

Time: About 4–5 hours to a week at camp.
Cost: From $10 to about $300.

See Local Resources: 2, 3.

---| 16 |---

Remember a Single Parent on Special Occasions

Did you ever wonder how a single parent gets a present from his/her child? Who remembers the single parent on Father's Day or Mother's Day? Do single parents get a Christmas present from their children? In two-parent families, Dad usually takes the kids to get Mom a special present, or Mom accompanies the son or daughter to find a gift for Dad.

With very little money and a couple hours of your time, you can perform this special task for a single parent—and bring many smiles.

Anne and Jim know a single parent through work. Her family lives some distance away and her son has no contact with his father. On Mother's Day and on Mom's birthday, a bouquet of flowers arrives for her, just to say, "We're thinking about you. Have a wonderful day!"

Gary and his wife Laurie adopt a single parent at Christmastime. They either buy the mother and children a gift, or they send gift certificates from local restaurants. Imagine what a treat going out to dinner can be for a single mom and her children!

With a few moments and very little cash, you can be a tremendous blessing to someone who may be badly in need of a little encouragement.

Time: About 30 minutes to an hour.
Cost: About $10 to $50.

See Local Resources: 2, 3.

---| 17 |---

Volunteer at Your Pregnancy Counseling Center

The newsletter of your local crisis-pregnancy counseling center may contain a list of volunteers and different skills needed. The centers are always looking for willing and dependable hands who can help answer the hotline phone, counsel young women, serve as a receptionist, clean the office, sort maternity and baby clothing, and perform a variety of other general tasks. Don't think for a minute that you must be a skilled counselor in order to be of service to your local center!

Brenda has taken on the task of organizing the baby and maternity clothes closet for her center. Once a week she comes in, cleans up any disorderly shelves from the previous week and sorts new things that have come in. If she receives used clothing that needs mending, she separates it for another lady who has volunteered her services in this area.

Ellen is badly crippled and needs to spend a great deal of time in bed because of the pain. She wondered what, if anything, she could do to make a difference in the pro-life cause. Then she received a newsletter from a pregnancy center in her area and saw they had a need for hotline counselors—a job that Ellen soon discovered could be done at home. The director of the center was delighted to have Ellen's services, and arranged for her training. Ellen is now one of their best hotline volunteers. Because of her disability she is often available when everyone else is busy, such as nights or during holidays. Her servant's heart has made a difference, not only in the women the center serves but in Ellen's life as well.

If you are interested in serving as a receptionist, or working directly with young women in a counseling setting, or on the hotline, most pregnancy centers will provide training and support. Many volunteers, however, prefer to come in a few hours a month to give their time in whatever way is needed. Working women and men can offer to serve on a board committee that meets less frequently, or come in one evening a month. This is an opportunity to take a few hours to make a difference in your community.

Time: As many hours as you like.
Cost: Nothing.

See Local Resources: 1, 2, 3.

| 18 |

Pass on Your Unique Gifts to Young Women at a Maternity Home

"I just love to do crafts, and I was wondering if you have any need for someone like me at your maternity home?" Anne enjoyed getting calls like this!

Volunteers who have special abilities are a tremendous asset to a maternity home, or to one of the single-parent programs being formed today. These volunteers help build the self-esteem of the young women, and provide them with a good use of their time. The family and friends of the young women are usually deeply touched by gifts that the young women have made themselves. Many of these women have knitted blankets, or made some special memento to send with their child whom they are placing up for adoption.

- Carl and Melissa had done ceramics for years. They volunteered to come to a maternity home once a week for six weeks and work with the women on special projects. It was getting close to Christmas, so they decided Christmas tree decorations would be in order. As the weeks progressed, ornaments were painted, then fired and brought back to the home. The faces of the young women lit up when they saw the finished products. Many of the ornaments were given away as Christmas gifts, but the house-parents were most delighted when they received a handmade, signed ornament from each of the young women in the home. They are still a priceless treasure in their home.
- Susan called to say she would be willing to teach the young women cross-stitching. She came for several weeks and gave lessons. Cross-stitching was everywhere!
- A piano teacher contacted a maternity home and asked if they had a piano. When she found out they did, she offered to give lessons one afternoon a week. The home paid for the music books and this woman donated the lessons as a gift. Many young women discovered a new talent and went on to continue the lessons elsewhere.

Maybe you are not especially gifted in crafts, but desire to help in this area. You can call your local maternity home and offer to buy materials for craft lessons. There is a constant need for needlework kits, balls of yarn or skeins of embroidery floss. Such simple, thoughtful gifts can make a permanent difference in some young woman's life.

Maternity homes also need childbirth instructors, women interested in teaching aerobics and exercise, and people able to teach about nutrition. Tutors in various scholastic areas are another area of need.

Time: A few hours a week.
Cost: Nothing to $50 or $100, depending on what you would like to donate.

See Local Resources: 1, 3.

19

Be a Foster Parent for an Adoption Agency

Many adoption agencies have a unique need: They are looking for caring couples who will take in newborn babies while they are awaiting adoption, or while their birth mothers are getting their thoughts and lives together.

Who is considered for foster parenting? A family in which the wife is at home is a must. It's ideal if she has experience with infants. And if she currently has young children, or has raised children of her own, this is also a plus.

When couples decide to be foster parents, they also choose to say goodbye. They realize the placement is only temporary, and most experience deep emotions when it is time to hand the child over to new parents or back to the birth mother. It is a very special ministry for very special people.

Sam and Betty have always loved children, and have a small extra room in their house. They contacted a local adoption agency several years ago and have since had more than twenty children live with them. Each child has held a special place in their lives.

When you visit Sam and Betty, they love to bring out their scrapbook and show you the wonderful children God has allowed them to care for. Some only stayed with them for a week or two; the longest they had a child was a year and a half. Each has been equally loved and nourished.

Foster parenting these special babies takes courage and lots of love. But those who are called to it know that their prayers and care have made a difference that will last a lifetime.

Time: Initial screening and training time (one or two in-service days); a few days to a few months per child.
Cost: Nothing. Generally, everything the couple needs is provided by the adoption agency. In some cases there may be minimal costs.

See Local Resources: 1, 3.

20

Serve on the Board of a Pro-Life Ministry

Every nonprofit organization must, by law, have a board of directors. Getting the right people to serve on the board, however, can be very difficult.

There are two main levels of service in this area. An individual can volunteer to serve on a particular committee, or to serve on the board of directors as a whole. Generally speaking, serving on the board is a greater commitment than serving on a committee, although involvement on a committee (such as a banquet, or a walk-a-thon committee) can be very intense for shorter periods of time.

- Alice is a homemaker with three children. She and her husband and family had recently moved back into their home area after having been away for several years. She called an old friend and, in the course of the conversation, found out that she was involved in a pregnancy counseling center that was just starting. Alice called the center to see how she could serve, too, and was told their greatest need was for board members. She filled out an

application, submitted it and, to her delight, found that she had
the right qualifications. Alice has made a valuable addition to the
board, which meets evenings while her husband sits with the
children.

- Rod and his wife are both retired and have extra time on their
hands. Over the years they have volunteered at a maternity home.
Now Rod is serving on the board and learning how the program
operates from the top to the bottom.

Boards of Christian ministries need godly people with all kinds of
gifts and abilities. The most important ingredient is a willingness to
serve and the time it takes.

Time: Two to six hours a month.
Cost: Nothing to a minimal cost.

See Local Resources: 3.

21

Talk to a Friend About Your Feelings

You might ask how talking to a friend can make a difference in the
pro-life movement. (Notice, the word is talk, not "argue.") It is amazing
how the smallest statement or piece of information given to the right
person at just the right time can change a heart forever.

Linda, a young woman from Ohio, recently told Anne how she became
involved in the pro-life movement. She was talking with a neighbor who
mentioned picking up material from her church to help her better understand the issue of abortion. The neighbor got the material for Linda
and gave it to her; then they continued talking about other things.

When Linda got home she laid the pamphlets aside for a while, and
even forgot she had them. But one day she picked up the material and
began to read. Her heart was deeply touched, and when she finished she
was in tears. She was even more moved than her neighbor by the pamphlets!

Linda is now actively involved in her local pro-life ministry and is feeling more fulfillment than she has ever felt in her life. She knows she is making a difference. All because someone else took the time to hand her a pamphlet.

Time: A few minutes to possibly an hour or two.
Cost: The minimal cost of a few pieces of literature.

See Local Resources: 3.
National Resources: 3, 6, 9, 14, 17, 19, 20, 22.

22

Help Your Child With School and Book Reports

Have you ever thought about how many school and book reports each child does by the time he or she graduates from high school? In college, the numbers of papers and reports is incredible!

Young people often come home from school with certain assignments and ask their parents help to pick out a book or material that covers the particular subject matter. Reading and reporting on a pro-life book is an excellent way to spread the message that everyone has value and is important in God's eyes. There are wonderful books at all age levels on abortion, adoption, pregnancy, the development of pre-born babies in the womb, handicapped children and adults.

Amy was a freshman in college, and was taking a class on debate. Each student was to choose a subject to debate and prepare their material. Amy chose to speak on abortion, and visited her local crisis pregnancy center for background material. They gave her more than enough material to work with, and even offered to make handouts for her entire class. She received an *A* on her paper. Afterward, a student came to her and confided that she had an abortion and was struggling with the emotional effects of what she had done. Amy was able to refer her to a post-abortion support group at the crisis pregnancy center.

Helping our children to understand the issues and to share them in the classroom prepares them to defend their views later as adults. It can also change their teachers' lives and the lives of the other students in the class. For a list of resources, see the Appendix.

Time: An hour to several hours, depending on the size and scope of the report.

Cost: Cost of book(s) if you can't borrow them or obtain them from a library.

See Local Resources: 3, 5, 6, 9.

23

Become Involved With Handicapped People

Any work with the handicapped is pro-life work. Handicapped people are special people in our society who bring a depth of courage and challenge into our lives, as well. Anne feels very strongly about this:

"As the parents of a handicapped young woman, Jim and I know firsthand how important it is to have people who are willing to include our daughter Shelly in their lives. Unless you have lived it, you have no idea how lonely it is to be handicapped and left out of so much. Our Shelly is always thrilled to be included in someone's plans. One couple invited her on a fishing trip. Another time, a single woman invited her to a dinner theater. Words cannot express the appreciation and encouragement Shelly felt. True, most handicapped people have some limitations that require extra help, but they can still be involved in activities. All they need is a sensitive person who will give some additional thought to their needs."

Becoming involved with a handicapped person does not require a great time investment. Involvement can be as simple as inviting them to sit with you at church, or taking them along with you to a social or church activity.

John was in an accident at age twenty, and now, three years later, he lives in a nursing home, paralyzed from the neck down and breathing with the help of a ventilator. Visits from people mean so much to him. John also collects baseball caps, so Jim tries to remember him when he travels. Getting a new hat adds to his day.

There is no question that the secular, as well as the Christian community, needs to do more to reach out to handicapped people and give handicapped people better access to buildings and events. But have you considered giving a handicapped person access to your heart? Joni Eareckson has founded a ministry that reaches out to handicapped people around the world. Information can be found in the Appendix.

Time: A few minutes, or possibly a few hours.
Cost: Minimal or none at all.

See Local Resources: 2, 7.
National Resources: 15.

$$\boxed{24}$$

Bake a Treat

Some people are blessed with the gift of being able to turn out home-baked goodies at the drop of a hat. If God has given you this gift, why not share it for the benefit of the pro-life movement?

You may want to call your local pregnancy center and offer to bring over treats for the volunteers. This serves very special people who are giving their time and talents to the center and is a way to encourage them in their work.

A woman in our community stops by our ministry office periodically to bring packs of crackers and cheese and cookies she has purchased. We are so blessed to feel a sense of God's love through her.

Another way baking can be a gift to the pro-life community is through holding bake sales. You can participate if your local ministry is having a bake sake or a fund-raising event that might require refreshments, such as an auction or flea market. If you have organizational abilities as well, you can organize a bake sale yourself, with the profits going to your favorite pro-life work. This allows other home-bakers to be involved also.

Young women living at maternity homes can always use a special treat, too. You can take them one of your favorite dishes and leave the recipe with them. Helping them make a great batch of cookies, a cake or another wonderful dish is a way to build a young woman's self-esteem. You could also offer to supply a cake when there is a special occasion, such as a birthday, graduation, or other event to celebrate.

Even if you are not a baker or don't have the extra time, you can visit your grocery store and occasionally take baked goods to the pregnancy counseling center or maternity home. Many baked items can be frozen for future events or special treats—and they will always be greatly enjoyed!

Hearts are encouraged through the gift of baking. Perhaps you can provide that source of encouragement to the pro-life community.

Time: Generally, a couple of hours per event, plus delivery time.
Cost: Ingredients for the recipe, or the baked goods themselves.

See Local Resources: 3.

$$\boxed{25}$$

Become the Pro-Life Contact Person for Your Church

If your church will permit, volunteer to be an advocate for the various pro-life ministries and needs in your area within your church body.

Most local pro-life ministries are looking for someone they can contact regularly with information about their prayer and volunteer needs, or news of upcoming banquets or events. It is much more effective for them to be able to use one individual from each church to get out news of their ministry to the entire congregation. This may require putting some of their newsletters on a literature table, writing a column for the church newsletter, getting items into the bulletin, or making some phone calls.

Being a church contact person involves keeping in touch with the ministries, reading their newsletters regularly, and being aware of their needs. If your area has several ministries, you might want to put a monthly flyer in the back of the church condensing all the ministries' needs and promoting upcoming events.

A contact person may also help their church become involved in fund-raising events by advertising, and by recruiting people to participate in walk-a-thons, bake sales, banquets and other events.

Although Becky had several small children at home, she found she could be the pro-life contact person for her church without ever leaving home. Each month she wrote a column for the church newsletter and made sure local ministries' newsletters and fund-raising events were publicized at her church. Becky's involvement and visibility helped others in her church become involved in pro-life work through the years. Her church is known today as a pro-life influence throughout their whole denomination.

Time: About an hour or two a month.
Cost: None.

See Local Resources: 2, 3.

26

Invite Someone From a Pro-Life Ministry to Speak

Many civic clubs or social groups have provisions for guest speakers as part of their regular programs. Sometimes they appoint a committee from their membership to invite the speakers, at other times they entertain suggestions from the entire membership. If you are a member of a civic group or service club, one way you can help spread the pro-life message and get recognition for pro-life ministries is by suggesting a pro-life speaker to the group or program committee.

Since pro-life ministries address critical social issues such as teen pregnancy, venereal diseases, sexuality, chastity and morality, to name a few, you might be surprised to find how receptive your local organization is to hearing what the ministry is doing about the problem. Many social service organizations vote on which nonprofit organizations in the community to donate their annual funds to each year, so you might even be the means by which a local pro-life group receives a monetary grant to help with their work.

Anne has spoken at many women's fellowships. Many of these groups have collected food and have had fund-raising projects for the ministry of Loving and Caring. As a result of Anne sharing, some individuals have also become supporters, birth coaches and volunteer counselors. Their hearts and lives were opened to this issue because someone invited Anne to speak.

Time: Very little.
Cost: None, or a small honorarium.
See Local Resources: 1, 3.

27

Invite a Pro-Life Speaker to Your School

There are many classes, especially at the high school level, where a presentation by a pro-life speaker would be appropriate—such as home economics, health, social studies and religion classes. Many of these speakers are invited because of a personal request from a student to his or her teacher.

Another way to help pro-life ministries get into public schools is to identify schoolteachers and guidance counselors in your church. You can approach these people with materials from local pro-life ministries, give them a list of resources they can obtain (videos, films, pamphlets), and tell them of the willingness of staff members to share with students. Many teachers are open to having speakers address their students, but don't have the time themselves to research available resources.

When Jim and Anne were houseparents, the students at a local public high school were asked by their religion class teacher to submit names of guest speakers they would like to hear and who could tell how they lived out their religion. Because of their full-time involvement in ministry, Jim and Anne were invited to share their lifestyle and work during the class. Not only were they able to explain why they had chosen to give their lives to the pro-life movement full time, but also about how they lived by faith and trusted God for their finances.

Some schools do not invite outside speakers, but teachers may be open to showing a video or distributing literature. Many pro-life ministries own videos on subjects such as the early stages of life, abortion, adoption and chastity, and they might be happy to loan them to your school. Some of the videos even have discussion guides or accompanying literature to share.

Over the years we have met many people who have changed their minds on the pro-life issue because a fellow student made the effort to see that the message was presented in school.

Time: About one or two hours to research materials from your pro-life groups; 15 minutes to talk to a teacher.
Cost: Nothing.

See Local Resources: 1, 3.

28

Help Make Young Women in a Maternity Home Feel Welcome

It is frightening to be pregnant, alone, and moving into an unknown living situation with strangers. This is what young women face the first days after they enter a maternity home. You can help make them feel at home and ease their transition by becoming involved in a ministry to welcome them.

One way this can be done is through welcome baskets. Welcome baskets can contain anything the person or group making them wants them to. One maternity home's volunteers put together a basket consisting of personal items—shampoo, toothbrush and toothpaste, makeup, hand lotion—to be distributed to new residents. Whenever possible the volunteers approach merchants and ask for donations of samples, then supplement with travel-size containers they purchase at a discount drugstore. Other ideas to include in a welcome basket are note paper and a few stamps, a pen, a candy bar, or an item for her hair, such as a barrette. The baskets are decorated and placed in the young woman's room on the day of her arrival.

Another home has a particularly artistic volunteer make pretty name plaques for each young woman's bedroom door. When she leaves, she may take her plaque with her.

Jim and Anne were blessed by a group of Mennonite ladies who made each young woman in their home a quilt they could keep. The young women were thrilled, and as the years have gone by, many of them still have their treasures.

Any of these ideas can make a new resident feel good about herself *and* help make her adjustment to her new environment a more pleasant one. Contact the director or houseparents of your local maternity home and ask if anyone is volunteering for this service.

Time: A couple of hours each month to collect items and assemble baskets. More time is needed to make quilts and other projects.
Cost: Depends upon your contacts.

See Local Resources: 3.

29

Give Financially

We don't want to overlook one of the major means that allows ministries to continue to serve: financial contributions. Without God's provision for these ministries through His people, they would be unable to continue the important services they offer to their community.

Some people like to give by designating funds for particular purposes, and in this book we've given suggestions for some designations. But ministries cannot function with totally designated funds. They also need a large pool of undesignated funding for heat and light, salaries and rent, phones and postage, all of which are necessary.

What does it take financially to run a counseling center or maternity home? Many pregnancy counseling centers are staffed with only one or two full-time people; some have no paid staff at all. In terms of expenses, the location of the center plays a crucial part. As counseling centers become more and more sophisticated in the services they offer, their budgets increase. We know centers that were started on a shoestring and are now operating on budgets of $60,000 to $75,000 a year or more, offering an abundance of services and resources to their community in lovely offices. Because maternity homes run a more intensive day-to-day operation, supplying food to a number of young women in larger buildings, operating twenty-four hours a day, they generally have larger budgets than pregnancy centers.

What about support for local offices of national ministries? Some people think that because an organization belongs to a larger national group, they are supported through the national office. Nothing is further from the truth! Even though a ministry may be nationally affiliated with, perhaps, Birthright, the Christian Action Council, or Bethany Christian Services, the local offices of all these groups are responsible for raising their own support for staff and for all operating expenses.

National offices of ministries have needs, too. They must maintain their offices, hire staff to oversee the local ministries, and bear the weight of huge phone bills as they keep in contact with their branch offices. One of the primary responsibilities of national offices is to develop materials, training seminars and resources for their local affiliates, and for the pro-life movement as a whole. This work is very expensive and is generally funded by contributions.

The majority of the funding for a pro-life ministry comes from the grass-roots support of Christian people like you who contribute small amounts of money on a regular basis—not from church budgets, foundations, or government grants. When Anne and Jim were at the House of His Creation, a maternity home, one woman who lived on a social security pension and whom Anne had met years before faithfully put $6 in cash in an envelope each month and mailed it to the home for its work. Another widow started the practice of putting a penny in a jar at every meal. Pro-life ministries such as maternity homes, adoption agencies, and counseling centers survive today because of widow's mites such as hers.

Pro-life piggy banks?

You can get your children involved in pro-life giving by placing a baby bottle on your kitchen table. Every meal, each family member places a nickel or a few pennies (or a penny for every year of one's life) in the bottle. At the end of the month, the proceeds from the bottle are given to a local pro-life ministry to help a woman and her baby. Another method you might use is to designate one particular coin for pro-life work. Every time a family member receives that particular coin in change, that coin goes into the bottle at the next meal. When it is full, the change is donated.

Time: Five minutes a month to write a check and address an envelope.
Cost: As much as you are able to give.

See Local Resources: 3.

30

Subscribe to Publications That Keep Your Family Informed on Issues

Like television, what comes into our homes in the way of reading material has an impact on our entire family. Are most of your subscriptions to Christian magazines? Do you receive a pro-life magazine in your home? We might find it hard to make a case for our cause if we don't have current facts and research on hand supporting our position. Fortunately, there is a wealth of information available for this in the form of excellent pro-life and pro-family publications.

Focus on the Family publishes several magazines that help families keep informed about Christian values and issues, including magazines for teens and *Citizen*, a monthly magazine about national issues. Most Christian magazines have a pro-life emphasis. Anne tries to give some of her favorite Christian magazines to friends as gifts.

Why not consider giving a Christian magazine as a gift to your

local doctor's office? One doctor recently told us that a patient sub-
scribed to Focus on the Family's *Physician* magazine for him. He
enjoys it so much he passes on his copies to physician friends.

Time: Negligible.
Cost: Varies according to the magazine. About $15 to $20 for each
magazine you give as a gift.

See National Resources: 2, 6, 8, 11, 14, 20, 22.

31

Make a Name for Yourself in the Media

If you have a strong opinion and can present yourself fairly well,
you are a candidate to express your opinion to the news media whenever a topic arises that touches an area relating to pro-life issues.

In the newspaper.

Probably one of the easiest ways to express your opinion is on the
editorial page of your local newspaper. Newspapers are generally eager
to publish letters to the editor from individuals who are moved to respond to a current event, or to editorials or articles they have published. The best letters are typed and make a clear, logical case for the
writer's position as briefly as possible. The more current the letter, the
better. (Don't respond to an article that was printed last week. No one
will be able to remember what it said.) A signature is imperative if you
wish to see your letter published.

One woman we know has taken on a personal mission of writing
letters to the editor of her local paper. Leslie, who was an English major
in college, tries to discern just the right issue to respond to, then
carefully constructs a thought-provoking letter to the editor. She tries
not to send them in too frequently so the paper won't disregard her as
a "regular." So far, every one of her letters has been published.

On TV or radio.

Currently there is no FCC fairness doctrine that requires equal time for differing points of view on radio or TV, although Congress is trying to reinstate the fairness doctrine. However, many radio and TV stations do have an informal policy regarding replying to their broadcast editorials. People who hold a differing point of view may come to the studio and tape a rebuttal. These rebuttals are then played on the air at the discretion of the station. When you check with your local station, they will tell you their policy and conditions regarding length. At this point you can, if you choose, make an appointment for a taping. We suggest you write out your rebuttal in advance and read it on the air.

If you disagree with a news station's editorial opinion or coverage of the pro-life position, and if the station's policy does not provide for the opportunity for a rebuttal, you should write the station manager, expressing your objection to their airing a single point of view. If they refuse to acknowledge your letter and refuse to change their coverage, you are within your rights to write them again, citing your previous letter, and send a copy to the FCC. If the FCC receives many letters of this type, they may take the station's fairness into consideration the next time they review their license.

Don't just criticize.

While most letters to the editor and editorial rebuttals disagree with the media's official opinion or policy, it is also good to be positive, writing to agree with them whenever you can, or to commend them when they take a stand for the value of life, the elderly or the handicapped.

Time: An hour or two.
Cost: Postage.

See Local Resources: 9.
National Resources: 2, 6, 8, 11, 14, 22.

32

Give a Party!

Everyone loves a party, and pro-life ministries are no exception! If you have a part-time position giving in-home parties for cosmetics, kitchenware, toys, stitchery, consider donating the proceeds from one of your parties to your local pro-life ministry.

You can host the party yourself, have a friend host the party at her home, or the party can be held at the pro-life ministry and combined with an Open House. Invitations are sent out to either specially selected friends of the ministry or individuals and friends of the party hostess. (It's always good when you can widen the circle of people who are aware of a particular ministry.) Proceeds from the party to the ministry range from 15 to 20 percent of the total sales. The "hostess gift," which is usually given to the person who hosts the party, might go to the ministry, if it's something they can use.

One Tupperware lady we met passed out catalogs to all her friends at area churches, who also passed them around. She committed to donate the proceeds from any items purchased from the catalogs during an entire month to a pro-life organization.

If you are in the party business, contact your local pro-life ministry and ask if they would be open to hosting a party in exchange for your donating the profits. The contacts you make might even be good for your business!

Time: The preparation time involved for a party, and one evening.
Cost: The proceeds from one evening.

Resources: Your own business, or your friends who promote parties as part of their part-time business.

See Local Resources: 3.

| 33 |

Be a Labor Coach for a Single Pregnant Woman

There is probably no process as lonely or painful as giving birth when you have no one there to support you. Many pregnancy centers and maternity homes rely on trained labor coaches to help their clients and residents through this special moment.

To be a labor coach, you need not be a nurse or even a mother yourself. You must have time to commit to attending childbirth classes with the young woman assigned to you, and must agree to be available for her when her time to deliver is near. The childbirth classes prepare both you and your young woman for the birth process and give you plenty of time to get acquainted. Having a birth coach gives the young woman another "special friend" she can count on while she is waiting for her baby to arrive.

Carol doesn't have children of her own and had never seen a "live birth" prior to the movie shown in her first childbirth class. The maternity home paired her with Cathy, a serious young woman who shared a lot of common interests with Carol. They became good friends while Cathy waited for her child to arrive.

Late one evening, Carol got the call that Cathy was experiencing contractions. She arrived at the hospital just as Cathy was brought there, and accompanied her up to the labor room. The labor was hard but blessedly short. Carol encouraged and prayed for Cathy, helped her with her breathing, and timed her contractions. When Cathy's baby was finally born, Cathy and Carol cried together. They held each other and cried again three days later as they dressed the baby, prayed for her safety, and placed her with an adoption worker so she could be turned over to her adoptive parents. Whenever Carol thinks of her first experience as a labor coach, she remembers Cathy and the precious time they had together.

The commitment to support a young woman through labor can be made as often or as infrequently as a coach wishes. But once the commitment is made for a particular women, the labor coach must do everything in her power to see it through to the birth. In the process, both parties will be blessed.

Time: Approximately 8 to 10 hours for childbirth classes, and from several hours to a day in the hospital during delivery. (Delivery may occur at any hour of the day or night, so schedules must be flexible.) Also count on extra phone calls, lunches, and/or visits with your young woman.

Cost: Maybe the cost of a couple lunches to become better acquainted with your young woman, a bouquet of flowers for the hospital, and possibly a baby gift.

See Local Resources: 3.

34

Mend/Make Clothing for a Pro-Life Ministry

Do you have a gift of sewing? Do you like to sew for others? Pro-life organizations frequently need the services of willing seamstresses.

One of the objectives of a pregnancy-counseling ministry, adoption agency or maternity home is to help supply the physical items necessary to enable the pregnant woman to carry her child to term. Sometimes this includes maternity clothing for herself and infant layette items for her newborn. These are obtained either new or used through donations. Used items occasionally need repair work.

Some ministries also operate thrift shops. Donations come in by the bag or truckload and need to be sorted and cleaned. Many items may need to be mended.

Single parents are often stretched financially. Hands that are willing to mend and sew can be a great gift. Handicapped people often need special alterations so that their clothing fits properly.

At the maternity home, a ladies sewing circle can always be kept busy making new items for both mothers and babies, including maternity tops, crocheted blankets and baby sweater sets.

For almost twenty years, Aunt May, a live-in volunteer at the House of His Creation, has given her willing hands to sew and mend clothing for the nine to fifteen girls who live in the maternity home Anne and Jim founded. One Easter, her sewing machine made outfits for every female member of the family as Aunt May personally saw that *everyone* had an Easter dress to wear to church.

Time: As much or as little as you have.
Cost: Minimal.

See Local Resources: 3.

35

Host a Baby Shower

What woman doesn't like to attend a baby shower and "oooh" and "aaah" over miniature booties and tiny dresses and bonnets? You could hold a baby shower *at any time*. Invite your friends over, play games, open gifts, eat, have an evening of fun—then donate all the shower gifts to a local ministry. These showers can be sponsored by individuals or by groups.

Pro-life ministries continually collect baby items to distribute to the young women in their care. This provides for a very real need and encourages her to carry her child to term. These items include receiving blankets, stretch suits, diaper bags, infant dresses and suits, sweaters, sleepwear, undershirts, and anything else a baby might need. You might want to include some information about the ministry you're helping, and/or invite someone from the ministry to attend and open the gifts. This is one of the ways you can introduce a friend to your local pro-life ministry.

While many ministries accept used items, it is always nice to be able to offer a young woman a few nice, brand-new items just for her child. At many maternity homes, each young woman receives a new outfit in which to bring the baby home from the hospital, or to dress the baby for its trip to the adoption agency. This new outfit is supplemented with a few other new items, as well as many used items from donations. A baby shower is one important and fun means you can use to collect the new clothing.

Time: Some planning/preparation time, depending upon how extravagant a baby shower you desire. One afternoon or evening for the shower.

Cost: About $10 to $20 for invitations and snacks, and $10 to $15 per gift.

See Local Resources: 3.

| 36 |

Organize or Participate in "Work Days" at a Pro-Life Ministry

We've already talked about the need for ministries to maintain their buildings, grounds, vehicles and equipment. Unfortunately, property maintenance can take valuable time away from their primary focus, which is ministry.

If you belong to a religious or civic group that can spare just one Saturday a year, you can provide an invaluable service. Many such groups look for projects that can benefit their community. A work day at a local pro-life ministry can be planned as one of these annual projects.

- One youth group offers a Saturday each season to help with yard work at a maternity home.
- An adult Sunday school class spends a day a year doing interior painting or outside yard work for a ministry, as needed.
- One Bible study group volunteered to raise money for wallpaper and then hung the wallpaper themselves during a work day.
- Work days can be used to repair a roof, plant a garden, clean windows, paint a barn, shampoo carpets, build an addition, remove a dead tree, and countless other tasks, both big and small.

As you can imagine, work crews take some advance planning. Call the ministry in advance and ask what projects need to be done. Coordinate an appropriate date for the work and discuss supplies they have on hand, as well as what supplies you'll need to bring with you.

You'll need to ask about food, as well. Some ministries are able to easily supply a lunch, while this would be hard for others. A three- to six-month notice for a workday is advisable. After the project and date are set, it's time to recruit and schedule the helpers.

The secret of a well-organized workday is that it takes a large task and divides it up among many enthusiastic people. You'll be surprised how much can be accomplished in a single day when many hands are involved. This is another opportunity to introduce some friends to a pro-life ministry.

Time: One day, plus some advance organization.
Cost: None, unless you would like to contribute for needed materials.

See Local Resources: 3.

37

Picket an Abortion Clinic

One very effective way to stop abortions at their source is to picket an abortion clinic on the days it is performing abortions. Many children have been saved from abortion when their mothers have turned back from entering the clinic because of seeing picketers, or when they were handed information by sidewalk counselors about alternatives to abortion. Many women choose abortion because they feel there is no other option, and are actually relieved to know that help and alternatives are available.

Who are these people who picket abortion clinics? They are from all branches of the body of Christ, young and old, single and married. They are steadfast, turning out in all types of weather. They share a common goal: to save the lives of innocent babies at the doorstep of the place where they're about to be killed.

There were no abortion clinics in Ed and Stephanie's area until 1984. But when a clinic was started, they and the members of their church decided that, as Christians, they could not let it perform abortions unchallenged. They started picketing on Saturdays and Wednesdays when the clinic does abortions and, along with individuals from other faiths, have been picketing for the last six years.

On the third Saturday of the month they get a large turnout of 50 to 100 people from all over the area. The other Saturdays and Wednesdays have a lighter turnout, but a handful of picketers and sidewalk counselors try to be available for the young women on those days as well.

During one of the pickets, the pastor of Ed and Stephanie's church approached a young couple who were about to go into the clinic. He talked to them about abortion and offered help if they needed it. They listened to what he had to say and that day decided to turn back from the clinic. A few months later the pastor received a Christmas card. It was from the young woman he had met at the clinic, and in it she told him she had decided to give birth to her child. The church got together and gave the couple a shower and the couple called several months later to let the pastor know the baby had been born. The pastor hopes the church will be able to continue to have a relationship with the young couple.

Ed and Stephanie estimate that at least one baby a month has been saved because of the efforts of the picketers at the abortion clinic. One baby a month from 1984 to 1990 equals 84 precious children who were allowed to live because people cared enough to spend Saturdays and Wednesdays picketing and praying.

Time: As often as you would like when your local abortion clinic is performing abortions.

Cost: None.

See Local Resources: 2, 3.

38

Investigate What Your Schools Are Teaching About Sexuality and Offer Them Alternatives

Do you have a clear idea what your school is teaching your child about sex? Do you know what textbooks are being used and what values they represent? Do you know what values your son or daughter's teacher presents in class? As parents, we try to instill godly values in our children—while forces in many schools are trying just as hard to see that your child's education is stripped of any Christian influences whatsoever.

Where do you start? If you have children in school and have established an honest and open rapport with them, you can start by asking them what they're being taught about sexuality. Ask them to share their textbooks with you. As parents, you can approach the teacher and ask to see copies of the curriculum being used. You can also attend school-board meetings and voice your opinion when issues arise that affect your child and your values.

One group in a medium-sized city formed "Respect Young America," a nonprofit organization with the purpose of making value-based resources available on chastity and sex education to the public schools. They have amassed a collection of video tapes on chastity that they loan free to teachers and guidance counselors and also show to parents and teens in churches. Their goal is to provide a positive response to the Planned Parenthood philosophy so prevalent in schools and to influence their schools to teach chastity as the basis of their sex education curricula.*

Time: A couple hours or longer, if you decide to start a group.
Cost: Depends upon your interests. There may be no cost at all.

See Local Resources: 3, 5, 6, 8.
National Resources: 1, 4, 6, 13, 16, 25, 26, 28.

---

*Planned Parenthood's philosophy of sex education and history of abortion can best be understood by reading the recent Planned Parenthood exposé *Grand Illusions: The Legacy of Planned Parenthood* by George Grant.

|39|

Sponsor a Pro-Life Writing Contest at Your Local Christian School

Because the *Roe* v. *Wade* Supreme Court decision was handed down in January 1973, January is "Right to Life" month. "Right to Life Sunday" falls on the Sunday in January closest to January 22. Many Christian schools like to sponsor a pro-life activity in January. It is a wonderful way to begin the new year with a pro-life message.

A businessman we're aware of approached his local Christian school and offered to sponsor a pro-life writing contest. Since the school went from kindergarten through high school, several divisions were formed. The different groups were instructed to write up to one full page on the following subjects:

First through third grade: "I am glad to be alive because . . ."

Fourth through sixth grade: "I am glad to be alive because . . ."

Seventh through ninth grade: "I am pro-life because . . ."

Tenth through twelfth grade: "The call to be pro-life can best be fulfilled in my life by . . ."

A panel was recruited to judge the papers. Gift certificates for $5, $10, and $15 from a Christian bookstore were awarded to the first three students in each division. The Friday before "Right to Life" Sunday, the winning papers were read at a school assembly and the students were recognized. On "Right to Life Sunday," the winning entries were reprinted in a booklet in the church bulletin.

Time: Approximately half a day to organize the contest.
Cost: $120 in prizes.

| 40 |

Write or Sponsor a Pamphlet

Jerri had an abortion and, years later, decided to put her feelings about it on paper. She showed Anne what she had written, and Anne knew Jerri's story would really be a help to others who had experienced the same thing. A pro-life couple from the community heard about the project, stepped forward and offered to finance the printing. The little pamphlet, *Overcoming an Abortion,* became a reality. So far, 31,000 copies have been distributed around the country and orders for it continue to come in.

Brochures containing personal testimonies need to be written, printed and distributed in order to help and bless others. But, often, the person whose experience can powerfully bless others is not in the position to fund the printing and distribution of her own testimony.

You can help by letting your pro-life ministry know you would be willing to participate in a printing project. Let them know what you would be able to donate to see that someone's personal story reaches a wider audience. So many ideas lie dormant simply because funds are not available. Bringing the kingdom of God to earth involves team work on many occasions.

Time: Very little.
Cost: $25 to $500, depending on the printing project.

See Local Resource: 3.

| 41 |

Walk or Sponsor Someone in a "Walk-A-Thon"

Actually, there are different types of "thons," from walk-, to bike-, to run-a-thons. There are even "rock-a-thons" in which participants rock in chairs for a set period of time. The common element is that individuals are spending several hours of their time to raise funds and make a difference for a pro-life ministry.

There are three ways you can participate in any "thon":

- You can volunteer to help with the planning and running of a walk-a-thon. Volunteers are needed to recruit and coordinate participants from different churches, to help with refreshments, to receive pledges, or to do the many other jobs required to make a walk-a-thon work.
- Participating in a walk-a-thon yourself involves contacting your church or pro-life coordinator, receiving the necessary paperwork, and signing up people to sponsor you—such as relatives, friends, church members, customers, teachers. Generally, there are prizes for individuals who, for instance, accumulate the most sponsors or the most money.
- You can participate in a "thon" by sponsoring someone else. This means agreeing to pay a participant a certain amount for each mile of the course the person completes. If no one has approached you to become a sponsor, you can still help by calling the sponsoring ministry and offering to be a sponsor. They'll be delighted to assign someone to you.

Brian, Sally and their two children all agreed a walk-a-thon was a pro-life project they could participate in together as a family. They decided each one would work to raise $100. When one went over $100, they would help another obtain pledges until the family had raised a total of $400. On the day of the walk they had a great time with the other walkers, and each member earned a $10 gift certificate. This, of course, led to another fun family outing!

Time: A few minutes to be a sponsor; three or so hours to participate; eight hours or so if you help coordinate participants from your church.

Cost: The amount you decide to sponsor.

See Local Resources: 3.

42

Talk to Your Doctor

Cindy directs a large pregnancy-counseling center in the South. One type of call the center receives is from women seeking referrals to pro-life physicians. Cindy's center recently referred Ruth to what Cindy thought was a pro-life physician.

Ruth, who had recently moved from out-of-state, made an appointment with the obstetrician. She asked if he did abortions. He said he did not, and neither did he refer women for abortions.

But during the examination he suggested that Ruth, who was 40, have an amniocentesis. "Why would you recommend that?" she asked. "Well," he hesitated, "at your age you never know . . . If there's anything wrong, well . . . it would be good to have a choice." The strong implication, of course, was that if her baby was found to be "not perfect," she may want to abort it.

Because she is strongly pro-life, Ruth shared her disappointment with him. Later, she called Cindy to ask for another referral. Sadly, Cindy says that after surveying the eighty-six doctors in their community, the center is able to refer women to only one physician whom they feel is committed to being pro-life.

What questions can you ask to be sure your doctor is pro-life? Some are:

"Do you ever refer women to Planned Parenthood?"
"Under what conditions would you recommend amniocentesis?"
"Do you do abortions?"
"Do your partners do abortions?"
"Do you make referrals for abortion?"

According to a pro-life physician we contacted, there are several pro-life, pro-fetus reasons a physician may suggest amniocentesis. One legitimate reason for amniocentesis is to determine the maturity of the baby's lungs in the event an early delivery is indicated. Another reason would be for women whose babies were at high risk for RH disease to determine the severity of the baby's problem. In some cases an inter-uterine transfusion could be performed, while in severe cases the risk of a premature delivery is less than the risk of carrying the baby to term.

A third, more controversial reason is when, like Ruth, a woman is in the high risk category (over 38 years of age) for delivering a Down's syndrome baby. Many physicians, even those who are strongly pro-life, feel an obligation to discuss the possibility of amniocentesis to determine if the baby will have Down's syndrome. While pro-life doctors would never recommend, or perform an abortion in such a case, many feel that *not* mentioning the test leaves them open to law suits. And some pro-life women, while they would not consider abortion, may want time to mentally prepare themselves and their families in such an eventuality.

Time: None.

Cost: The inconvenience of finding another doctor if yours does not have a pro-life stance.

See Local Resources: 3.

43

Shop Garage Sales/Thrift Stores

Maternity homes and pregnancy-counseling centers have a need for a wide range of baby items and furniture. They give these items to their clients who cannot afford to buy them for themselves. Occasionally, used infant furniture is donated.

Purchased new, the cost of items such as cribs, highchairs, car seats, infant seats and playpens is prohibitive. But if you frequent garage sales and thrift shops for your family (or just for the fun of it), you may be able to find an occasional item at an inexpensive price, then donate your find to your local pro-life ministry.

If you make a point of telling the seller that you intend to donate what you purchase to a home for unwed mothers or a group that counsels single pregnant women, they may reduce the cost further, or even be glad to give it to you "for a good cause."

Time: No additional time. You only need to keep your eyes open as you shop.

Cost: Whatever "deals" you can arrange with the seller. Keep in mind that anything you donate that you paid for is tax-deductible.

See Local Resources: 3.

44

Participate in or Start a Pro-Life Sunday at Your Church

If your church does not currently observe a "Pro-Life Sunday," you may want to ask your pastor if he is willing to let you help start one. Many Catholic churches observe this event on the first Sunday in October, which is "Respect Life Month."

- One way to observe "Pro-Life Sunday" is by placing pro-life pamphlets in your church bulletin. For several years, the Christian Action Council (see Appendix A under National Resources: 6) has been supplying beautiful color bulletin inserts for "Pro-Life Sunday" to churches on request. The National Council of Catholic Bishops also supplies posters and bulletin inserts for "Respect Life Month."

- Another way to make this day pro-life is by having a sermon from your pastor or an invited speaker based on some aspect of abortion or respect for life. (Appendix C is a list of scriptures that can be used for a pro-life message.)

- Inviting a speaker, or showing a video on pro-life issues in youth/adult Sunday school classes is another way to give this Sunday a pro-life emphasis.

- One group we know polls all the pro-life ministries in the county before "Pro-Life Sunday" and compiles a list to distribute to the congregation. The list includes the names, addresses and phone numbers of the ministries, the type of work they do, and their current needs.

- At least two churches in our area take up a special collection for the pro-life movement. This collection is divided among the pro-life ministries in the area.
- Another idea is to have a literature table in the back of church with brochures from all the ministries in your area and pro-life books available from your church library.

Time: A few hours a year to research and gather material.
Cost: The cost of bulletin inserts, or the cost of copying and distributing your own information.

See Local Resources: 2, 3, 5.
National Resources: 5, 6, 24.

45

"Back Up" Houseparents

Those who serve full time as houseparents of maternity homes need to count on having time off to refresh themselves physically and spiritually and to pull together as a couple or family. Many maternity homes have policies giving houseparents time off on a weekly or monthly basis, in addition to vacation time. The universal problem of these homes is how to find people willing to fill in for them. Volunteering to relieve a set of houseparents is something you can do as a couple, as a family, or as a single woman. It's a special blessing when relief houseparents are able to fill in on a regular basis, because it gives young women in the residence familiar faces to become comfortable with in their houseparents' absence.

Serving as relief houseparents requires a willingness to be a servant to the ministry, to abide by whatever rules have been established by the administration and the present houseparents, and an eagerness to show God's love to each of the girls. Most ministries will have their own criteria for relief houseparents. Because of space considerations, some will only consider couples or singles. Others may have room for entire families. Most (for obvious reasons) will not accept couples with teenaged sons. Ministries that take minors (girls under 18) may be required by law to fingerprint and run a police check on volunteers, including relief houseparents. Some states require relief houseparents to complete a Red Cross CPR course. Many ministries have an orientation program for relief houseparents that includes instructions on whom to call and what to do in different emergencies.

Most frequently, being a relief houseparent involves overseeing the young women's schoolwork and meals, possibly leading a brief devotional time, seeing that they get to church on time on Sunday, and maybe playing games or watching TV in the evening or going out for an ice cream treat together. Weekend housesitters will usually not have the responsibility of sitting for a full house, since several young women will probably be visiting their families on any given weekend.

Darlene started out as a volunteer driver for a maternity home, taking young women to their doctor's appointments. As she began to interact with the young women, she felt the Lord leading her to become more involved with them. She asked to be a labor coach and began accompanying them into the delivery room. Then she and her husband volunteered to be "back ups" for the present houseparents. They now spend several weekends a year in the home with the young women. The more Darlene becomes involved, the more she wants to do.

If being a relief houseparent appeals to you, call your local maternity home. They'll be glad to tell you if they have a need and what their criteria are for relief houseparents. Those who have volunteered in this area say the blessings they received through the experience were as great as those given to the houseparents by having the time off.

Time: Anywhere from an evening, to a weekend, or one to two weeks.
Cost: No cost to the relief houseparents. Any expenses should be handled by the maternity home.

See Local Resources: 3.

---| 46 |---

Help Your Church or Pro-Life Group Sponsor a Sexuality Seminar

Helping young women in crisis pregnancy acknowledges that an error has already been made. It deals with *effects*. Sponsoring a sexuality seminar can be a preventive measure, addressing one of the *causes*.

Pro-life issues and sexuality issues are tied together by the biblical belief that all life is created by God and that when parents produce a child, they involve themselves with God's plan. Sex outside of marriage has been seen to have dire consequences in just one generation. Teenage pregnancy and abortion is one sad consequence. Venereal diseases and AIDS are others. In this country, as more fatherless children are brought into the world, we see lawlessness increasing both in our streets and in our culture.

The fact that pre-born infants are precious and worthy of life represents one side of the pro-life belief; another side is the sacredness of married love between a husband and wife. This is a message that needs to reach our Christian young people.

One way to get the message across is to approach the youth leaders at your church about hosting a sexuality seminar for youth and, possibly, their parents. There are many excellent video series, study materials and books available to help a group get the chastity message across. Many communities also have trained speakers who may be willing to talk to your group.

One pregnancy center held several two-day sexuality seminars for young people in their community. The seminars featured national and local speakers, contemporary Christian music, and a sleep-over on Friday evening. Teens from the center's supporting churches attended, paying a minimal fee. Their parents were invited to attend a three-hour session on Saturday morning. The center found that the seminar was well received by the young people in their community, and it plans to hold another one.

Time: Planning a well-run sexuality seminar and getting the word out to young people requires quite a bit of advance planning by a committee of people. Plan on several months of preparation.

Cost: There may be costs involved, depending upon your speakers and materials. These costs can be defrayed with private contributions, or through a grant from a ministry or church.

See Local Resources: 2, 3, 8.
National Resources: 1, 4, 6, 16, 25, 26, 28.

$$\boxed{47}$$

Organize or Participate in a Life Chain

Life Chains, consisting of Christians standing silently holding signs that read "Abortion Kills Children," started as a California movement. It was the idea of Royce Dunn, a businessman who also directs a pro-life ministry, as a creative way to motivate the Christian community. The first known human Life Chain in 1987 was located in Royce's rural community and consisted of 2500 residents. In 1989, Life Chains were taken across the state. In San Diego last spring, 28,000 people turned out for a Life Chain that stretched 15 miles!

The idea of Life Chains is taking hold across the country as a peaceful, nonthreatening means of Christians uniting for the unborn. The movement cuts across all different denominations and has been instrumental in unifying diverse churches in the communities where Life Chains take place. It has the approval of many different pro-life organizations as a valuable means of getting more people involved in the pro-life movement. The key to a successful Life Chain is prayer and church recruitment. The San Diego Life Chain, for example, included participation by 200 churches.

There are plans for a National Life Chain in 1991 or 1992 in which millions, it is hoped, will participate. But in the meantime, Life Chains are the product of local communities. A Life Chain packet is available, consisting of a manual, video, and the rights to duplicate both in each community. The material can be used to help a group recruit pastors and churches.

If you hear of a Life Chain being organized in your community, why not plan on taking a couple hours on a Sunday afternoon to participate? If there is nothing planned, perhaps you could be the initiator of a Life Chain that tells your community and your political representatives that many, many people care about the unborn.

Time: Several hours to participate in a Life Chain. Approximately three months to effectively organize one.

Cost: No cost to stand in a Life Chain (a freewill donation may be taken). Costs for hosting a successful Life Chain vary, but can be underwritten by churches, businessmen, or individuals. The total cost for the Life Chain of 28,000 people in San Diego was $4,000.

National Resources: Royce Dunn
Please Let Me Live
3209 Colusa Highway
Yuba City, CA 95993
(916) 671–5500

48

Compile a List of Materials and Resources for Your Denomination

Catholic churches are parts of Dioceses, Presbyterian churches are members of Presbyteries, and Methodist churches belong to Conferences. If you belong to a denominational church, you might want to consider how your church can bring the pro-life message and pro-life resources to other area churches in your denomination.

Andrea, who belongs to a Presbyterian church, wanted to do more to impact her denomination. She discovered her denomination has a national pro-life group called Presbyterians Pro-Life. After contacting them she found that one of the things she could do was influence her church to become a "Resource Center for Abortion Alternatives." To do this, she had to find other people in her church who were willing to help, get her pastor and elders' permission, then write a letter to her local Presbytery, asking that her church be designated a Resource Center.

Andrea's group then researched all the pro-life ministries in the Presbytery, such as adoption agencies, pro-life centers and counseling ministries, post-abortion support groups and maternity homes. They compiled a list and sent it to the pastors of the other churches in their denomination. They also included all the resources available such as speakers and videos from these ministries that could be presented to small groups. This provided these pastors with referral options that were both Christian and pro-life and alerted them to local ministries that need their church's support. Although Andrea did this for her Presbyterian denomination, this information could be researched and provided to pastors of *any* denomination. Unfortunately, many denominational pastors are more familiar with Planned Parenthood than they are with local pro-life ministries.

During the course of their research, especially in small communities, individuals from a church may find that there are no local ministries meeting the needs of women in their care with crisis pregnancies. Because of this, many churches have started their own counseling centers and support services.

Becoming a pro-life influence in its denomination is one way a church can fulfill the biblical mandate to "defend the cause of the weak and fatherless" (Psalm 82:3).

Time: Having your church become a pro-life resource center requires a group of committed people meeting on a regular basis and several hours of research each month.

Cost: The costs involved are postage, envelopes, paper, and the cost of copies to first survey local ministries and then send a list to area pastors. Starting a pregnancy counseling ministry under your church requires a greater commitment of time and funds.

See Local Resources: 3.
National Resources: All that are listed.

| 49 |

Show a Pro-Life Film or Video to Your Church or Youth Group

At Loving and Caring, we've had the opportunity to talk to pro-life people from all over the country. Anne meets them as she travels and when they come to the retreats we hold twice a year. Carol writes about them in articles in Loving and Caring's newsletter. And we're frequently on the phone with them throughout the week as they consult with us or place orders.

With all of our contacts across the nation, we've discovered a pattern as to how these dedicated people first became involved in the pro-life movement. A great majority of them (many more than what could be discounted as "coincidence") are active in pro-life work today because several years ago they had the opportunity to see the powerful film series by Francis Schaeffer: "What Ever Happened to the Human Race?" In many cases, the number of people at the viewing was small, in fact, a disappointment to the sponsoring church or group. Completely unknown to the film's sponsors, however, God was moving through this series to raise up an army of committed pro-life workers.

This underscores the importance of introducing your friends to pro-life movies and videos. Although the "crowd" may be small, you have no idea who may be touched to do great things for the kingdom of God as a result of seeing a single film.

Today, there are many films available that can be obtained through a loan from a pro-life group, through rentals, or purchased outright. Don't underestimate the possibility that hearts may be stirred to action by this simple tool.

Time: A couple days to research availability and prices.
Cost: Varies greatly, depending upon whether you want to borrow, rent, or purchase films. (Some of the costs may be recovered by charging a small admission fee or taking up a free-will offering.)

See Local Resources: 3.
National Resources: 2, 6, 9, 11, 19.

50

Start a Civics Committee at Your Church

Bob and a group of four other men began a civics group in their church five years ago. The purpose was to keep their large, active congregation informed of pro-life and political issues and encourage their participation. Any information of a political or pro-life nature that comes to their pastor is automatically referred to this group, which is responsible for determining its value to the congregation and getting out the word to other members.

Since they started, the group has accomplished the following helpful services:

- They held voter registration drives and made absentee ballots available.
- They have rented buses for the March for Life in Washington and encouraged people to attend.
- They have produced local county voter's guides before each election. Bob firmly believes that Christians haven't been voting simply because they didn't know whom they were voting for, especially at the local level. The civic group's voters' guide polls everyone running for office, asking candidates basic information about their views, and publishes it in a nonpartisan manner. "If someone stands for biblical values, we find that people *will* get out and vote."
- They have made their congregation aware of decency/pornography issues. The group believes that the secret of any effective grass-roots movement is making it as easy as possible for people to get involved. When the American Family Association decided in 1989 to boycott two national advertisers that were supporting violent shows on TV, the civics committee asked the church's printing department to print a postcard to the chairman of the board of the offending advertisers. The card was included in the church bulletin. Anyone who wished to support the boycott was asked to fill out the card and drop it in the collection basket. Over 1000 cards were mailed in from members of this congregation alone! Because of response from Christians around the country,

one of the two advertisers has since dropped its sponsorship of violent and sexually explicit programs.

• They have sponsored a permanent display in the foyer of the church. The display includes pamphlets on various issues; copies of *Forerunner*, a news tabloid with a Christian message that motivates people to become involved; names, addresses and photographs of state and national representatives; and prayer concerns.

• They have placed announcements in the bulletin regarding political bills that require action or letters to their representatives. One of the goals of the committee is to have a group of 10 or more people from the congregation who are willing to write their senators and congressmen regarding their support of pro-life and pro-family issues. "If every church could motivate just 10 people to regularly write their representatives, they would be overwhelmed with mail representing Christian values."

Bob says one proof that involvement is working is a recent county election. A Christian candidate defeated a pro-abortion incumbent who had held a state representative post for 18 years. The Christian vote was a deciding factor in the victory.

Time: A few hours a month to start and run a civics committee.
Cost: Office supplies as needed.

See Local Resources: 4.
National Resources: 2, 3, 6, 8, 10, 11, 13, 14, 22.

51

Enhance Self-Image, and Make a Memory

There are different ways we can be sensitive to women who have decided to carry their baby, even though the circumstances are not what they would prefer. Many women facing a crisis pregnancy suffer from low self-esteem. Coping with the last months of pregnancy is hard enough for any woman without facing the rejection of your boyfriend and sometimes even family and friends.

One way to boost the self-image of a young woman in this tough position is to help her feel good about herself. Young women in a maternity home need to exercise and eat right if they're going to have the safest and easiest delivery possible. If you are gifted in leading low-impact exercise or aerobics classes, you can offer to run a series of classes for your local maternity home or pregnancy center. It's a good way to get the young women mingling, moving about, laughing together and establishing friendships with you and each other. And, hopefully, the pattern of exercising will be one that stays with them after they have their child.

Enhance their femininity. Do you do color analysis? Are you a makeup consultant? Are you gifted in nail care? Do you give professional haircuts or perms? All these gifts contribute to helping a young woman feel better about her appearance.

Elaine, a makeup and color consultant for Amway products, is glad to donate her time to help young women feel good about their appearance. Pregnancy counselors from her area know they can call her if they are counseling a client who needs an extra lift and advice about colors and clothing. Elaine also donates any extra samples of makeup that she uses in her consultations to a maternity home in her area.

Linda volunteers her professional manicure services to unwed mothers free of charge as a way of giving them an extra treat they would not otherwise have.

Say it with flowers or food. Having a baby is a special time for most mothers and is usually accompanied by lots of flowers, cards, phone calls and well-wishers. This is not always the case when the child is the product of an unplanned pregnancy. It's especially hard on a young woman if she is rooming with someone whose half of the room looks like a florist's shop.

If you know of someone who is experiencing a crisis pregnancy, and if you're financially able, try to make a point to see that she receives flowers while she's in the hospital to show that someone cares.

If you don't know of a young woman, you might call a pregnancy counseling center or maternity home and offer to finance their efforts to send bouquets to birthmothers of their choice. Years later, many young women who received cards or flowers in the hospital during a crisis pregnancy still treasure their vases and notes—and the loving thoughts that came with it.

When Tammy was living in a maternity home, a visitor happened to stop by and strike up a conversation. The talk turned to favorite foods, and Tammy said that her absolute *favorite* was cheesecake with cherries on top! The visitor tucked that in the back of her mind and later called the home's secretary to ask to be notified when Tammy's baby was born. Sure enough, when the baby arrived the lady sent Tammy a whole cheesecake with cherries. Tammy still remembers the thoughtful Christian lady who sent her such a delicious gift.

Time: A few minutes to send a card or flowers; longer if you are going to give a manicure or makeup consultation or volunteer to lead aerobics or exercise classes.

Cost: Nothing for your time; $20 to $30 to send flowers.

See Local Resources: 3.

52

Remember Senior Citizens

We don't want to neglect the very important closing stages of life. There are a multitude of ways you can help and affirm the senior citizens in your life.

Are they widowed and alone? You can call them to check on their needs, invite them to celebrate a holiday with your family, take them out to dinner, offer to help them around the house, take them treats, invite them to accompany you to church, offer to help them shop or do their shopping for them, or send your children to play board games with them for an afternoon.

Are they in a nursing home? You can still take your family to visit, send cards and notes, pray for them and with them, and remember them on their birthday, special occasions and holidays.

Are you handy around the house? There are a variety of things that need to be done any time we are maintaining our own homes—and more, it seems, when we're not as agile or energetic as we used to be. If you have gifts in this area, you can help with minor repairs, grass-cutting or pruning chores and home winterization projects. One church recently got a group of men from their congregation together to put a new roof on a couple's home as an "80th birthday" surprise. Individuals donated money for the badly needed roof, the group took off the old roof and replaced it with a new one, and women from the church helped serve refreshments during the day.

Time: Varies, depending upon the projects you select. The time you spend can involve a few minutes to address a card or note, to an afternoon for visiting or shopping. The entire roofing project took a group of men less than a day!

Cost: Also varies, depending upon the project you select.

See Local Resources: 2, 7.

Part Two:
Things Requiring More Involvement

53

Start a Support Group for Women Who Have Had Abortions

Jerri had an abortion, and afterward experienced depression, anger and an obsession with babies. Counseling helped her to see that her emotional problems stemmed from the abortion. As Jerri now says, "I came to understand that I didn't feel God was punishing me enough for what I did, so I was trying to punish myself."

Now married and the mother of three boys, she attended a pro-life convention in her city in 1982 and signed up with the local chapter of the Christian Action Council. "I put off doing anything with the CAC until about a year later, when I attended one of their meetings. There, a doctor addressed the group and said, 'I see a lot of women with emotional scars from abortion. I feel as a Christian organization we should consider starting a support group for women who've had abortions.' "

Jerri's ministry was born that night. She collected information on the subject from WEBA (Women Exploited by Abortion), was listed in WEBA's state catalog, and started receiving calls from around the state to speak. This public-speaking experience proved invaluable once she began her support group.

Planning the support group took Jerri a little over a year. When it was ready to start, she called it "H.O.P.E. for Life." H.O.P.E. stands for

"Helping Overcome Past Experiences."

At H.O.P.E. for Life meetings, Jerri makes use of the PACE workbooks for women who have had abortions, videos, and tapes from seminars and conventions. "I share right away that I am not a counselor, but that I have a list of pastors and Christian counselors who can help them if they feel the need for further help outside the support group.

"When I started, I thought I'd have to do all the talking," says Jerri. "But the members themselves usually come up with the topics. As new women come to the group, we go back over some familiar material. Since most of us have been through that phase, we're better able to help the next person."

Jerri's ministry today reaches beyond the H.O.P.E. for Life support group. She receives calls from around the state to speak, as well as from women who need to talk to someone who understands what they've gone through. "Sometimes I can be on the phone counseling for several hours," Jerri says, "but it's always worthwhile to see lives changed through forgiveness and God's love."

Time: Several hours a month to prepare material for the support group; speaking time is additional, as is time on the telephone.

Cost: There may be some cost for brochures and refreshments at meetings, but these may be picked up by a local ministry willing to sponsor the group.

See Local Resources: 3.
National Resources: 6, 18, 23, 27.

54

Consider Adopting a "Special Needs" Child

There are thousands of couples waiting to adopt "normal" newborn babies. But there are thousands of special-needs children waiting for homes. These children may be handicapped in some way, they may be older, or they may be part of a sibling group who, for various reasons, must stay together.

Beth, a professional woman, is single and loves children. She has recently adopted three boys from the same family. The youngest is four and the oldest is fourteen. There have been some adjustments, but after a year, everyone seems to be doing fine. Beth has found children to pour her love into, and the boys have found a wonderful mother to love and nurture them.

Joe and Mary, who were unable to have children of their own, have adopted three special-needs children. Today their lives are full of adventure. The children are filling Joe and Mary's household with activity, love and life. Special challenges arise daily, but they are always met with victories, because of this couple's commitment and God's love spilling forth in their lives.

Time: A lifetime.

Cost: More than we can imagine—but so is any type of child-rearing! (Some special-needs children are eligible for government subsidies.)

See Local Resources: 1, 3.
National Resources: National Committee on Adoption
1930 17th St. NW
Washington, DC 20009
202–328–1200

55

Be an Extended Family to a Young Woman in Need

Over the years, dozens of young women who were pregnant and in need came to live with Anne and Jim. Their two girls were brought up living in a maternity home surrounded by a large "extended family."

An extended-family ministry can be carried out in your own home. It involves "extending" your family to include someone else. Many crisis pregnancy centers and maternity homes across the country desperately need homes of this type. Most provide training, and emotional and spiritual support while a young woman is living with you.

Who are the young women in need of a home? Many of them are

teens or young adults. A few of them have children and need a place for themselves and their child.

Anne and Jim's daughters, now grown, have developed lifelong friendships with some of the young women who once lived with them. They have learned what it means to care for others. The question Anne is asked most frequently by couples who are considering opening their home is this: "How will this affect our children?" Her reply: "If the Lord is leading you into this area of ministry, He's leading your children as well. How can caring for someone else with the compassion of Christ ever hurt?" Sometimes we are so busy giving our children what we *think* they need that we forget to teach them to care for others, producing a society of people who feel the world owes them comfort and happiness.

Anne also says, "I'm asked: 'Would you raise your children in an extended-family setting if you had to do it all over again? Do you have any regrets?' My only regrets are those of any parent who is not perfect and makes mistakes. But one mistake Jim and I didn't make was to have a family that lived only unto itself. *Yes*, I would do it again!"

Truly, extended-family living can represent Christ to hurting and wounded people. If you want to learn more of Jim and Anne's experience as an extended family, including practical information on how to live in an extended-family setting, the Appendix gives details for purchasing their true story, *Mending Hearts, Mending Lives.*

Time: Four to six months is an average stay.
Cost: Additional food, electric, water bills.

Resource: *Mending Hearts, Mending Lives,* by Anne Pierson, is a book about her family's experience as an extended family. It can be purchased from Loving and Caring (see Appendix, #21).

See Local Resources: 3.

56

Run for Political Office

If we as Christians want to have some voice in the operation of our country, we're going to have to step out in faith and put ourselves in positions of governmental leadership. Today, some of the more influential local positions in terms of pro-life decisions are the school board, the township supervisor and the county commissioners. In some states, the position of sheriff or deputy sheriff is also a very influential position.

The local school board. Whoever serves on the school board has great impact on our young people. School-board members make decisions on sex education curricula, school-based health clinics, the position school nurses and teachers will take in referring a pregnant student for an abortion, and many others. How do you become elected to the office of school-board member? Although it varies from state to state, most local activists agree that you should first be attending school-board meetings regularly, be reading your newspapers and be knowledgeable about the issues.

A person who wants to run for school board should first seek the endorsement of his or her party. This is done by contacting your local Democratic or Republican committee chairman and asking him or her for the party's endorsement. Something that might help you at this point is sending a letter to each committee member, telling them that you are interested in running and what you feel you have to offer the school board. Be prepared to meet with them and answer their questions before you receive any endorsement. If after several attempts you do not receive any interest from the political party, you can always have yourself placed on the ballot as an independent candidate without a party endorsement, but you would be running against the odds.

After receiving the committee endorsement, you must get a petition from the court house and accumulate the required number of signatures before you can be placed on the ballot in the primary elections. The number of signatures varies from state to state.

County positions. The township supervisor is another important position. Township supervisors have it in their power to grant or deny building permits for new business opportunities, such as abortion clinics. Someone seeking to run for township supervisor will go through a process similar to the person running for school board, asking for his or her party's endorsement, collecting signatures on a petition, and having his name placed on the primary ballot. This position is also used as a springboard for other political activities, such as county commissioner.

County commissioners choose which agencies receive county money and which are shut out from county funding. A strongly pro-abortion county commission will be sending monies to Planned Parenthood, while a pro-life commission will be interested in funding agencies that do not promote abortion.

The best way to find out about what is available at the county level is to call the Voter's Office at your county court house to find out when the terms are up for the position you are seeking. You can ask at that time how many signatures you will need on the petition. In Pennsylvania, most candidates are interviewed and selected by the political committees in January or February for a May primary. If your state's primary is earlier than May, you will need to pursue an endorsement before the beginning of the year.

Run for governor? In 1990 in Pennsylvania there was no candidate pro-life voters could support for governor in the Republican primary elections. At the last minute a pro-life housewife, Peg Luksik, who was not well-known outside the Christian community nor supported by the state Republican party, got enough signatures to be placed on the ballot. With very little financing and media coverage, and support only through churches and pro-life groups, she ran in the primary election and received 46 percent of the vote against her well-financed pro-abortion opponent, making national headlines and sending powerful signals to the state party.

Time: Varies widely, depending upon your staff and support. Running for office at the higher level, however, involves a full-time commitment during the campaign.

Cost: Also varies greatly. Peg Luksik's campaign for governor ended in the black!

See Local Resources: 4.
National Resources: 8, 10, 11, 22.

57

Plan a Pro-Life Career

Abby has almost completed a four-year degree in nursing, with an emphasis on obstetrics. Her interest in the field came as a result of a crisis pregnancy her older sister experienced. Abby became her sister's labor coach and helped Margaret through the delivery of her baby. The experience touched her so much that she now wants to devote her career to maternity care nursing.

If you are young and interested in seeking a position working full time in a pro-life field, it pays to investigate the requirements before planning your college education.

Evaluate your strengths. If you feel that you would be a good counselor in a maternity home, first call or visit the director of a local maternity home that is licensed by the state to see what the state requirements are. For instance, many young people assume that a counseling degree is needed to be a counselor. In fact, many states require a counselor in a maternity home to have at least a bachelor's degree in social work. Some may even require a master's degree in this field. If you like what you hear, ask the director to give you the names of some individuals in the field. Visit them and ask them questions before you choose your course of study.

Are you strong in business administration? Ten years ago, no one heard of a pregnancy counseling center or knew what it did. But we believe they are here to stay. If *Roe* v. *Wade* is reversed, or limited on a state-by-state basis, pregnancy centers will take on an even larger importance as women who were able to easily obtain abortions find they must now seek alternatives. And as maternity homes and pregnancy centers become larger, there will be a need for people with degrees or skills in business management and fundraising on staff to help direct these ministries. This is another area you might want to explore as you plan your career.

If you don't know exactly what you want to do, talk to someone who is working in a pro-life area. Tell them what your interests and strengths are and ask what kind of jobs might be available for you in pro-life work. They might be able to recommend courses of study and even specific schools where you can pursue your education.

There are many "secular" careers that greatly need pro-life professionals. Journalism, the medical profession and the legal profession, to name a few, desperately need the balance of articulate pro-lifers.

Time: It may take several hours or even days/weeks to research and plan your career. The time will not be wasted.

Cost: Phone calls, postage, transportation.

See Local Resources: 1, 2, 3, 7.
Some of the National Resources in your area of interest may also prove helpful.

| 58 |

Consider a Career Change

If you were a child of the fifties, sixties, or early seventies, you were educated in an era that wasn't even aware of the pro-life movement. The good news is: it's not too late to change the course of your career should you desire to do that. No experience is ever lost on God.

Carolyn's college degree is in home economics. She taught high school for several years, then left teaching for food service management. For the last three years she has served as director of a pro-life housing program for single parents and their children. In this capacity, she manages a nonprofit ministry that involves teaching young women about housing, food preparation, menu planning, budgeting, child development, and child care. "I've never had a position that tied together all of my work experience like this one does," Carolyn says. "Even my experience helping my father build homes years ago has come in handy. Most important, I'm involved in changing people's lives."

As Executive Director of the Christian Action Council, Tom Glessner oversees all of its extensive programs and operations, including 150 chapters and over 400 crisis pregnancy centers. Tom came into pro-life work from a legal background. He graduated from the University of Washington Law School and served as a practicing attorney for ten years in the Seattle area. As a self-employed attorney, Tom was able to devote part of his practice to the pro-life cause. He helped pro-life groups incorporate, did tax work for them, and represented pro-lifers in civil litigation. In the early eighties he helped found a crisis pregnancy center in the Seattle area, which, under Tom's leadership as chairman of the board, grew to four locations.

When Curt Young, the former executive director of the Christian Action Council, was making plans to leave CAC in 1987, he approached Tom about replacing him. Tom was reluctant to leave Seattle, but decided to submit his resume to CAC's board of directors. As it became clear that he was the CAC's leading candidate, Tom says he made the decision that he could always go back to law, but if he refused to walk through the door God was opening for him, he might be turning his back on an opportunity that would never come up again. He and his wife moved from Washington state to Washington, D.C.

Carol holds a communications degree and worked in the newspaper and magazine profession for fifteen years. Now full time at Loving and Caring, she helps Anne write and publish materials for groups that work with women experiencing crisis pregnancies, and also designs and writes all the brochures promoting Loving and Caring's retreats and publications.

Time: The time it takes to make contact with, or research positions in, the pro-life field.
Cost: There may be a financial cost to serving a Christian organization rather than serving in a secular position.

See Local Resources: 1, 2, 3.
A national organization that serves as a match-maker between Christians and ministry opportunities is:

> Intercristo
> 19303 Frement Avenue North
> Seattle, WA 98133

| 59 |

Serve as Houseparents in a Pro-Life Housing Ministry

We saved this one for one of the last because of the enormous commitment it involves on the part of a couple and their family. Houseparents "live" pro-life commitment twenty-four hours a day, seven days a week.

Who become houseparents? The field is open to any couple with servants' hearts who love and understand young people and who yearn to show them Jesus' forgiveness, love and compassion.

- Paul and Wilma had raised their three children when they accepted the position of houseparents in Florida. Their background included working with young people and running a Christian school as missionaries in Jamaica.
- Steve and Margie are a couple in their early forties. They became houseparents several years ago when their adopted son was four.
- Jerry and Kathy are parents of three children, the youngest just three. They moved across the country because they felt God's call on their lives to work with young people.
- Bob and Donna have grown children and grandchildren, but now are parents to a revolving family of young women.
- Both Darlene and Goldie, single women, chose to share their lives with women experiencing a crisis pregnancy by working in housing ministries in the Midwest.

Most houseparents reside on the grounds of the ministry, some in separate apartments, others in bedrooms adjacent to the young women they are serving. Their official capacity is to be "moms and dads" for a brief period to young women who may be temporarily estranged from their families, or who may not have any adults in their lives who are positive role models.

Their duties involve those of any Christian parents with a household of teenagers: seeing that chores are done, schoolwork is completed, meals prepared, buildings and grounds maintained, guests welcomed, and that unconditional love is abundant. Sometimes houseparents also serve as directors of the ministry, while in larger ministries with multiple homes, a director may oversee several homes and houseparents. Through God's grace, some houseparents thrive so much in the environment that they are still active and enthusiastic five and six years after they have begun. Others choose to commit a particular period of time to houseparenting: two or three years is standard.

All employees of a nonprofit ministry are accountable to a board of directors. In state-licensed homes, they are also accountable to a state licensing agency. So in the midst of maintaining a "homelike atmosphere," houseparents must keep the accurate and complete records required by their state.

One of the joys of houseparenting is that of seeing young lives permanently turned around, taking an entirely new direction from the one in which they were formerly headed. Another joy is being able to model for young women God's roles for the family. Still another joy is the special relationship houseparents occasionally share with a delightful young woman, so much so that the pain of letting go can be intense.

Is houseparenting for everyone? No. But for those who are called, it offers one solution to a much-needed home mission field—our country's own young people.

See Local Resources: 3.
National Resources: 7.

Loving and Caring: Who Are We?

Loving and Caring is a Christian organization that provides resources and materials to life-affirming groups and ministries. It was formed in 1984 by Jim and Anne Pierson, who saw the need for such an umbrella organization while they were directing the House of His Creation maternity home.

Loving and Caring first started by publishing *My Baby and Me* counseling workbooks for women in crisis pregnancies. To date, over 80,000 copies of the books have been sold to individuals, pro-life ministries, hospitals, and pastors. These workbooks were followed by numerous manuals for use in pregnancy work: maternity home manuals, extended family living, parenting class, counseling and fund-raising manuals were written to meet the unique needs of pro-life ministries. Anne Pierson's book *Mending Hearts, Mending Lives,* written for couples interested in opening their homes to unwed mothers, explores the eleven years she and her husband spent housing pregnant women at the House of His Creation. All in all, Jim and Anne Pierson have personally lived with approximately 200 young women.

The Christian Maternity/Single Parent Home Association is a ministry of Loving and Caring started in 1986. The CMHA brings together Christian maternity homes and single parent programs from around the country, publicizes them to pro-life counseling ministries and gives them an annual forum to meet and share their trials and triumphs.

Today, as Executive Director of Loving and Caring, Anne Pierson travels, giving seminars and retreats for staff and volunteers in the pro-life movement. Loving and Caring also hosts two annual retreats in Pennsylvania each year for those currently in, or interested in, pro-life ministry. Anne speaks at numerous fund-raising banquets for pro-life organizations and is also a speaker for Christian family camps, women's retreats and churches, where she shares from her many experiences the goodness and faithfulness of God in her and her husband's lives.

If you would like Loving and Caring's current price list and order form, information about starting a group home, having Anne speak, or a brochure on one of our upcoming retreats, please write us at:

1817 Olde Homestead Lane
Ste. H.
Lancaster, PA 17601

May God bless you for your prayers and efforts on behalf of His wounded children. If you have been involved in pro-life efforts we have not mentioned in this book, please write to us concerning your ideas.

Appendix A

Local Resources

1. *Your Phone Book.* The phone book is a good vehicle to find pro-life resources. If you are looking in the White Pages, you need to know the name of the ministry. If your phone book has a Guide to Human Services (generally blue pages), you can look under:

   Adoption Services
   Agency, Special Services
   Pregnancy Services
   Self-Help Support Groups

   If you are looking in the Yellow Pages you may want to look under:

   Abortion Alternatives
   Adoption Services
   Human Service Organizations
   Social Service Organizations

2. *Your Pastor or Local Pro-Life Church.* If your church is pro-life, your pastor will probably know of needs and ministries that would welcome your help. If you are not attending a pro-life church, contact a pastor and/or church in your community that is pro-life.

3. *Your Local Pregnancy Center/Maternity Home/Adoption Agency.* It is important to make sure that your center/home/agency is pro-life. When you make contact ask if they recommend abortion as an alternative to an unplanned pregnancy. Some people have become involved in what they thought was a "pro-life" ministry, only to find out later it was pro-abortion.

   After you have determined that they are pro-life, mention the specific areas in which you would like to serve. Feel free to make an appointment to visit the center/home/agency.

4. *For Political Involvement.* If you have a pro-life politician in your area, he/she would be an excellent resource for locating pro-life political groups.

   Other resources would include the local pro-life pastor/s, your local pro-life pregnancy center, maternity home, or adoption agency. They will usually know of pro-life political interest groups in your area.

5. *Your Christian Bookstore.* Generally, Christian bookstores are pro-life and carry some pro-life material. If there is a particular book, video or record that you want which they do not carry, they will be happy to order it for you.

6. *Your Local Library.* The number and selection of books available varies according to the librarian and the governing board who selects books. Usually you need to know the specific title to locate a desired book or other resources. If you notice a lack of material in this area, feel free to request it or donate it.

7. *Local Special Interest Groups.* To volunteer for services to the handi-capped and/or senior citizens, you may want to check your local phone book or newspaper. Many newspapers carry a section weekly that lists various support groups (i.e. Meals on Wheels, etc.). Your pastor may have knowledge of an individual who could benefit from your special services.

8. *Sex Education/Sexual Issues.* Your local pregnancy center, maternity home and/or adoption agency usually will have some resources in this area. They may also be aware of any groups or other interested people who are working or desire to work in this area. They can usually rec-ommend material that would be able to give you additional information.

9. *Local political/Pro-life School Issues.* Your local newspaper.

National Resources

1. AIDS Information Ministries
   P.O. Box 136116
   Fort Worth, TX 76136
   817–237–0230
   Resources, Newsletter, Videos

2. ALL About Issues
   American Life League
   P.O. Box 1350
   Stafford, VA 22554
   703–659–4171
   Magazine, Material, Resources

3. American Citizens Concerned for Life
   P.O. Box 179
   4000 Leslee Curve
   Excelsior, MN 55331
   612–474–0885
   Books, Flyers, Pamphlets

4. Bethany Christian Services/Bethany
   Productions
   901 Eastern Avenue NE
   Grand Rapids, MI 49503
   616–459–6273
   Books, Videos, Pamphlets

5. Birthright
   686 North Broad Street
   Woodbury, NJ 08096
   1–800–848–5683
   Resources

6. Christian Action Council
   101 W. Broad Street, Suite 500
   Falls Church, VA 20046
   703–237–2100
   "Action Line," Books, Videos,
   Pamphlets

7. Christian Maternity Home
   Association
   1817 Olde Homestead Lane, Suite H
   Lancaster, PA 17601
   717–293–3230
   Manuals, Cassettes, Resources

8. Concerned Women for America
   370 L' Enfant Promanade SW, Suite
   800
   Washington, DC 20024
   202–488–7000
   Magazine, Books, Resources

9. Easton Publishing Company
   P.O. Box 1064
   Jefferson City, MO 65102
   314–635–0609
   "How to Present a Pro-Life Program,"
   Books,
   Videos, Pamphlets

10. Family Research Council
    601 Pennsylvania Avenue NW,
        Suite 901
    Washington, DC 20004
    202–393–2100
    "Washington Watch," Books,
        Pamphlets

11. Focus on the Family
    Pomona, CA 91799
    714–623–0791
    *Citizen, Physician, Focus on the
        Family* Magazines,
    Youth Magazines, Cassettes, Books,
        Videos, Films, "Focus on the
        Family Resource Guide"

12. Heritage House '76 Inc.
    P.O. Box 730
    Taylor, AZ 85939
    602–536–7592
    Precious Feet Pins, Bumper Stickers,
        Buttons, Balloons, Decals

13. Human Life Center
    University of Steubenville
    Steubenville, OH 43952
    614–282–9953
    Pamphlets, Resources

14. Intercessors for America
    P.O. Box 2639
    Reston, VA 22090
    Pamphlets, Books, Videos, Resources

15. Joni and Friends
    P.O. Box 3333
    Agoura Hills, CA 91301–5012
    Books, Pamphlets, Resources

16. Josh McDowell Ministry
    P.O. Box 1000
    Dallas, TX 75221
    Materials, Resources, Videos, Books

17. Last Days Ministries
    Box 40
    Lindale, TX 75771–0040
    214–963–8675
    Pamphlets, T-shirts, Resources

18. Last Harvest Ministries, Inc.
    13604 Midway Rd., Suite 183
    Dallas, TX 75244–4305
    1–800–422–4542
    Materials, Books, Resources

19. Life Cycle Books
    P.O. Box 420
    Lewiston, NY 14092–0420
    416–690–5860
    Pamphlets, Books, Stickers, Buttons,
        Videos

20. Living World
    2606 ½ W. 8th Street
    Los Angeles, CA 90057
    Living World Magazine, Videos, Pro-
        Life Directory

21. Loving and Caring
    1817 Olde Homestead Lane, Suite H
    Lancaster, PA 17601
    717–293–3230
    Books, Pamphlets, Videos, Resources

22. National Right to Life
    419 7th Street NW, Suite 500
    Washington, D.C. 20004
    202–626–8820
    Newspaper, Books, Pamphlets,
        Resources

23. Open Arms
    P.O. Box 19835
    Indianapolis, IN 46219
    317–359–9950
    Materials, Resources

24. Pearson Institute
    3195 S. Grand Blvd. #A 2nd
    St. Louis, MO 63118
    314–652–5300
    Resources, Materials

25. Project Respect
    P.O. Box 97
    Golf, IL 60029
    Resources, Curriculum

26. Teen Aid Inc.
    W. 22 Mission
    Spokane, WA 99201–2320
    Materials, Resources

27. WEBA (Women Exploited By Abortion)
    24823 Nogal Street
    Moreno Valley, CA 92388
    714–924–4164
    Pamphlets, Resources

28. Womanity
    2141 Youngs Valley Road
    Walnut Creek, CA 94596
    Pamphlets, Resources

Appendix B

52-ITEM LIST

Below is a list of 52 grocery items regularly used in housing programs (some items used frequently have been duplicated). Keep this list in the kitchen near your shopping list. If each individual or member of a group would purchase and collect one item per week at the supermarket, it would be a great help to your local housing program.

Week   *Food/Supplies Needed*

1 • Canned fruit juices
2 • Cereal
3 • Mayonnaise
4 • Canned vegetables (no home-canned)*
5 • Steel wool pads
6 • Cake mixes
7 • Cake frosting
8 • Canned fruit (no home-canned)*
9 • Chocolate chips
10 • Kitchen cleanser
11 • Toilet tissue
12 • Popcorn
13 • Cereal
14 • Paper towels
15 • Dishwashing detergent
16 • Paper cups
17 • Canned tuna
18 • Applesauce (no home-canned)*
19 • Powdered drink mixes (lemonade, ice tea, etc.)
20 • Canned juices
21 • Ketchup
22 • Tissues
23 • Dishwasher powder
24 • Liquid bathroom cleaner

Week   *Food/Supplies Needed*

25 • Laundry detergent
26 • Maxi-pads
27 • Mayonnaise
28 • Rice
29 • Napkins
30 • Paper plates
31 • Paper cups
32 • Laundry detergent
33 • Kitchen cleanser
34 • Canned fruit (no home-canned)*
35 • Cereal
36 • Salad dressing
37 • Mini-pads
38 • Pudding mixes
39 • Plastic trash bags
40 • Paper towels
41 • Toilet tissue
42 • Pancake syrup
43 • Tomato sauce
44 • Tomato paste
45 • Window cleaner
46 • Canned tuna
47 • Fabric softener
48 • Jelly (not homemade)*
49 • Canned fruit
50 • Laundry detergent
51 • Hot chocolate mixes
52 • Sugar

---

*State regulations do not allow residents of housing programs to consume donated home-canned food items.

Appendix C

Key Scriptures Concerning Abortion

The Christian's concern with abortion is three-fold: concern for the baby, the mother, and our society.

The fact that the word "abortion" does not appear in the Bible does not mean God is silent on the subject. Rather, one must probe the Scriptures in a deeper and broader context to discern His will regarding this matter. One doesn't find "heroin" mentioned either, but it is not difficult for Christians to decide that its use is wrong. The basic question which must be answered is whether God deems the unborn to be a person. If the answer is "no," then perhaps we have the right to dispose of a fetus as an unwanted appendix or tumor. If the answer is "yes," then as Christians we must treat the unborn with all the love and concern due another person that God requires of us.

God knew David as a person before he was born, as related in Psalm 139:13–15. "For thou didst form my inward parts, thou didst knit me together in my mother's womb . . . Thou knowest me right well; my frame was not hidden from thee, when I was being made in secret. . . ." Human life begins at conception, for the Psalmist David uses the personal pronoun "me" in the above passage.

More directly, God speaks to Jeremiah, showing that the child in the womb is a person. "Now the word of the Lord came to me saying, 'Before I formed you in the womb I knew you, and before you were born I consecrated you . . .' " (Jeremiah 1:4–5).

The entity in the womb is a baby. Luke 1:41–44 says "And when Elizabeth heard the greeting of Mary, the babe leaped in her womb; and Elizabeth was filled with the Holy Spirit and she exclaimed with a loud cry, 'Blessed are you among women, and blessed is the fruit of your womb! And why is this granted me, that the mother of my Lord should come to me? For behold, when the voice of your greeting came to my ears, the babe in my womb leaped for joy.' " The Greek word for babe (brephos) as used in the Greek scriptures also denoted a baby in Luke 2:12–16; an infant in Luke 18:15, and a child in 2 Timothy 3:15. In these passages, we see that no distinction was made between born and unborn children.

The following concerns John the Baptist in Luke 1:15, ". . . he will be filled with the Holy Spirit, even from his mother's womb."

God knows the personalities of the unborn in Genesis 25:23, "two nations are in your womb" (Jacob and Esau) "and two peoples, born of you."

And Paul writes in Galations 1:15, "But when he who had set me apart before I was born, and had called me through his grace. . . ."

In these passages, God is dealing with the unborn. One He consecrates, another he sets apart for service, a third He fills with the Holy Spirit. Clearly, in these instances the unborn is a person. Lest there be any reservation that these may be special cases, consider the most unique person of all, our Savior Jesus Christ. Unique as He is, the Scriptures tell us that in His human nature He was to be like us in every way. Hebrews 2:17 says "Therefore he [Jesus] had to be made like his brethren in every respect, so that he might become a merciful and faithful high priest in the service of God. . . ."

From the moment of conception to the day He died on the cross, Jesus lived in humaness like you and me. There is no question of Jesus' personhood before birth. John 1:1, 14 tell us, "In the beginning was the Word, and the Word was with God, and the Word was God . . . And the Word became flesh and dwelt among us. . . ." Therefore, we too are persons from the moment of conception. By taking on the form of man, the Son of God has given man inestimable value. No exception can be made because of our size or shape or where we reside. We are indeed precious in God's sight and we must also be precious in each other's sight.

The passages in Proverbs 24:11–12 are especially fitting for us from this point on: "Rescue those who are being taken away to death." Can these be the unborn children who have no defense except our Christian conscience? The Living Bible Version of Proverbs 24:11–12 says, "Rescue those who are unjustly sentenced to death; don't stand back and let them die. Don't try to disclaim responsibility by saying you didn't know about it. Hold back those who are stumbling to the slaughter." Can these be the distressed parents who see abortion only as the deceptively simple answer to their problems? "If you say 'Behold, we did not know this,' does not He who weighs the heart perceive it? Does not He who keeps watch over your soul know it, and will He not requite man according to his work?" Can this mean us? With God's help and in Christian love, we can correct this situation.

Supplementary Scriptures

Where do the unborn come from?

"In the beginning God created the heavens and the earth" (Genesis 1:1).

". . . God created man in his own image" (Genesis 1:27).

". . . the children whom God has graciously given your servant" (Genesis 33:5).

"Thou hast granted me life . . ." (Job 10:12).

". . . the Lord granted his prayer, and Rebekah his wife conceived" (Genesis 25:21).

"[Children] are a heritage from the Lord, the fruit of the womb a reward" (Psalm 127:3).

When does life begin?

Throughout Scripture, conception has marked the beginning of an individual's life.

"And the woman conceived; and she sent and told David, I am with child" (2 Samuel 11:5).

". . . and she conceived and bore a son . . ." (1 Chronicles 7:23).

"And behold, your kinswoman Elizabeth in her old age has also conceived a son . . ." (Luke 1:36).

How does God view the abuse of children?

"And they forsook all the commandments of the Lord their God . . . And they burned their sons and daughters as offerings . . . Therefore the Lord was very angry with Israel and removed them out of his sight . . ." (2 Kings 17:16–20).

"The Lord said to Moses . . . Any man of the people of Israel, or of the strangers that sojourn in Israel, who gives any of his children to Molech shall be put to death" (Leviticus 20:1–5).

"They built the high places of Baal . . . to offer up their sons and daughters to Molech, though I did not command them, nor did it enter into my mind, that they should do this abomination . . ." (Jeremiah 32:35).

". . . I will not revoke the punishment; because they have ripped up women with child . . ." (Amos 1:13). God's law to Moses specifically covered the life and body of the unborn child in case of accidental damage by struggling men (Exodus 21:22–24). Jeremiah 7:6, 22:3, and Exodus 23:7 all state "Shed not innocent blood."

"There are six things which the Lord hates . . . haughty eyes, a lying tongue, *and hands that shed innocent blood.*" (Proverbs 6:16–17).

"Whoever sheds the blood of man, by man shall his blood be shed; for God made man in his own image" (Genesis 9:6).

"Thou shalt not kill" (Exodus 20:13). Murder is wrong according to: Matthew 5:21, 19:18; Romans 1:29; Revelation 21:8, 22:15.

"Whoever then relaxes one of the least of these commandments and teaches men so, shall be called least in the kingdom of heaven . . ." (Matthew 5:19).

"See that you do not despise one of these little ones; for I tell you that in heaven their angels always behold the face of my Father who is in heaven" (Matthew 18:10).

What about a "right to my own body"?

"Do you not know that your body is a temple of the Holy Spirit within you, which you have from God? You are not your own; you were bought with a price. So glorify God in your body" (1 Corinthians 6:19–20).

What does God say about the unfortunate who are deformed or sick?

"Woe to him who strives with his Maker, an earthen vessel with the potter! Does the clay say to him who fashions it, 'What are you making'? or 'Your work has no handles'? Woe to him who says to a father, 'What are you begetting?' or to a woman, 'With what are you in travail?' " (Isaiah 45:9–10).

"Because these experiences I had were so tremendous, God was afraid I might be puffed up by them; so I was given a physical condition which has been a thorn in my flesh . . . Three different times I begged God to make me well again. Each time he said, "No. But I am with you; that is all you need. My power shows up best in weak people" (2 Corinthians 12:7–9, TLB).

"No temptation has overtaken you that is not common to man. God is faithful, and he will not let you be tempted beyond your strength, but with the temptation will also provide the way of escape, that you may be able to endure it" (1 Corinthians 10:13).

"It is God himself who has made us what we are and given us new lives from Christ Jesus; and long ages ago he planned that we should spend these lives in helping others" (Ephesians 2:10, TLB).

"Always and for everything giving thanks in the name of our Lord Jesus Christ to God the Father" (Ephesians 5:20).

What if a person has been involved in an abortion? God forgives.

"If we confess our sins, he is faithful and just, and will forgive our sins, and cleanse us from all unrighteousness" (1 John 1:9).

"What shall we say then? Are we to continue in sin that grace may abound? By no means! How can we who died to sin still live in it?" (Roman 6:1–2).

"Dear brothers, if a Christian is overcome by some sin, you who are godly should gently and humbly help him back onto the right path, remembering that next time it might be one of you who is in the wrong" (Galatians 6:1, TLB).

What does Jesus expect of His church?

"Teacher, which is the greatest commandment in the law? And He said to him, 'You shall love the Lord your God with all your heart, and with all your soul, and with all your mind. This is the great and first commandment. And a second is like it, You shall love your neighbor as yourself. On these two commandments depend all the law and the prophets' " (Matthew 22:36–40).

"Then the righteous will answer him, 'Lord, when did we see thee hungry and feed thee, or thirsty and give thee drink? And when did we see thee a stranger and welcome thee, or naked and clothe thee? And when did we see thee sick or in prison and visit thee?' And the King will answer them, 'Truly, I say to you, as you did it to one of the least of these my brethern, you did it to me' " (Matthew 25:37–40).

"He who says, 'I know him' but disobeys his commandments is a liar, and the truth is not in him; but whoever keeps his word, in him truly love for God is perfected. By this we may be sure that we are in him: he who says he abides in him ought to walk in the same way in which he walked" (1 John 2:4–6). Jesus was confronted with a multitude of desperate situations, yet not once did He solve the problem by eliminating the person. This is the way in which He walked.

"You are the light of the world. A city set on a hill cannot be hid" (Matthew 5:14). This light gives the world its direction. We have an obligation to pronounce the truth, for we know in John 8:31–32, "If you continue in my word you are truly my disciples, and you will know the truth and the truth will make you free."

The Christian should follow God's laws, not man's.

"Do not be conformed to this world, but be transformed by the renewal of your mind, that you may prove what is the will of God, what is good and acceptable and perfect" (Romans 12:2).